THE

ART OF
LAWYERING

ESSENTIAL
KNOWLEDGE
FOR BECOMING
A GREAT
ATTORNEY

Paul M. Lisnek

sphinx
publishing

Copyright © 2010 by Paul M. Lisnek
Cover and internal design © 2010 by Sourcebooks, Inc.
Cover design by Kim Adornetto
Author photo by Maria Ponce Photography

Sourcebooks and the colophon are registered trademarks of Sourcebooks, Inc.

This publication is designed to provide accurate and authoritative information in regard to the subject matter covered. It is sold with the understanding that the publisher is not engaged in rendering legal, accounting, or other professional service. If legal advice or other expert assistance is required, the services of a competent professional person should be sought.
—*From a Declaration of Principles Jointly Adopted by a Committee of the American Bar Association and a Committee of Publishers and Associations*

All brand names and product names used in this book are trademarks, registered trademarks, or trade names of their respective holders. Sourcebooks, Inc., is not associated with any product or vendor in this book.

Published by Sphinx Publishing, an imprint of Sourcebooks, Inc.
P.O. Box 4410, Naperville, Illinois 60567-4410
(630) 961-3900
Fax: (630) 961-2168
www.sourcebooks.com

Library of Congress Cataloging-in-Publication data is on file with the publisher.

Printed and bound in the United States of America.
VP 10 9 8 7 6 5 4 3 2 1

For my family, who supports me unconditionally, and for my clients and audiences, who encourage and inspire me.

Contents

Acknowledgments

I have always believed that the most fascinating part of the law is to be found in the skills and techniques that constitute the art of lawyering. My work, writing, and teaching emphasize that the practice of law means paying attention to the human component of the case. Our victories come from understanding the power of persuasion, the ability to shape credible realities, and a dedication to the ethical practice of law. By adding a bit of humor and a cast of characters, I hope to highlight that the topics presented are drawn from experiences we have every day in court, in the office, and in life. Each column is drawn from some lawyer somewhere, some colleague's war story, or some strategy that has proven itself to be valid and reliable over time. Some forty columns later, it appeared worthwhile to bring the pieces together and offer them to you in an organized and structural fashion.

From the fictitious law firm of Mertz, Maude, and Matthews to the cast of lawyers who enter its doors, I pay tribute to the lawyers and special people who are part of my life... and you know who you are.

The many newspapers and journals that publish my column and the wonderful reader responses that come from lawyers, judges, and professors throughout the country would not be a reality without the trust and opportunity for me to test it all out in the cases for which I am retained as a trial consultant. It is with great admiration that I extend my warm appreciation to all my clients. Special mention must be made of those relationships that have transcended the years and many courts of law...your support has been my motivation to grow. Above all, thanks to Brian Lozell; Mertz and Matthew Lisnek-Lozell for putting up with me in all my craziness; Janet Contursi and our dear children, Alexandra Rose and Zachary Paul; my dear parents, Seymour and Sandy Lisnek, and my brother Rick and his wife; my sister, Judy Kien Lisnek, and the kids, David (Peanut), Michael (Pumpkin), Danielle, and Jackie; Ron and Ruth Lozell and the gang in Florida; Linda Kenney Baden and Dr. Michael Baden for their extraordinary efforts in writing the foreword for this book; Judge Haskell and Kay Pitluck; my team: Anne Brody Elovic, Diana Briggs, Zachary Johnston, Laura Kody, Bob Sandidge, Ronnie Rosenblum, and Richard Anton for immense support for my seminars and programs; my colleagues at Comcast and CN100 Network: Rebecca Cianci, producers Fred Prigge, Fernando Garron, Rich Foresman, Aaron Nowakowski, and Virginia Gordon, Nancy Bayless, and Lisa Aprati and Brenda Arelano; my colleagues at WGN-TV, with special thanks to anchor Larry Potash, News Director Greg Caputo, Associate News Director Jennifer Lyons, as well as Sandy Pudar, Jackie Keenan, Mike Wilder, Frava Burgess, and Maureen Wolf for all their support; my WVON radio team: Melody Spann Cooper, Jim O'Connell, Charles Twilley, Rey Diaz, and Mr. Michael Peery; my colleagues at Decision Analysis, the nation's leading jury and trial consulting firm, with special note to my partner Richard Gabriel; and for keeping me on the keynote speaking circuit, my speaking agents Brian Palmer, Don Jenkins, and Susan Masters and the support team at National Speakers Bureau, the country's number-one bureau; friends and colleagues at BarBri Bar Review, the nation's leading bar review prep course for whom it is my honor and pleasure to lecture on professional responsibility and constitutional law, among other topics, Richard and Melanie Conviser, Sherry Beattner, Stephanie and Charles Goetz, Mike Zavvy Sims, and Betsy Snyder; the gang at National Student Leadership Conference led by Rick Duffy (and Karen), and to Sandy Maldonado; dear friends Lady Wendy, Lord Michael, Sir Charles, Crosbie Marchant, Dr. and Mrs. Dan Ross, Jackie McCauley and Ray Lyle, Cindy Raymond, David Rittof, Randy and Becky Mathis, Theresa and Parker Ehrhart, Steve and Marla Cowan, Dottie and Jerry Fugiel-Smith, Richard and Eve Primus, Al Menotti (and Donut), Tim A. Jones, Marie Grabavoy, Helen Marcelino, Mommo, and Allen and Leann Almquist; and thanks to the memory of dear Maude, whom I loved so very much.

Thank you, my many clients, with special mention of Nikki Calvano of the United States Department of Justice and the Justice Leadership Institute, Rick Slee of the Ohio State Bar Association, Bill Hunt, Paul Alston, Louise Ing, Cori Lau, and David Nakashima, Dan Scheiss, Howard Zlotnick, Bob Chapman, Benji Haglund, and others who are kind enough to trust in my judgment and work on the cases that we tackle together, with appreciation for everything and for our agreement that the importance of communication is paramount in the practice of law. I thank you for your loyalty and friendship.

Enjoy the journey.
Paul M. Lisnek
March 2010

Foreword

RUSH to read Paul Lisnek's new book, *The Art of Lawyering*. If you do, you can become a great, *gr8* attorney!

If you want to be a great lawyer, your future depends on the ability to analyze and predict situations, then formulate strategies and responses through settings and language in order to present the most truthful and persuasive argument. Master this, and you too should experience success around the office, in the public eye, and especially in the courtroom.

Words have meaning. What you say, as well as how you say it, will trigger reactions; and how the person (or jury) listening to you reacts is of vital importance in achieving your goals.

Having worked closely with Dr. Paul Lisnek, his trial consulting partner Richard Gabriel, and their firm Decision Analysis, we have learned that the initial theme you present to your listener, along with their initial view of you, can shape many things. If you're capable, you can control which facts, ideas, ideals, and emotions you impart to your audience, giving yourself a major advantage in any public forum.

In this foreword, we are using the skills we learned from reading Paul's book, along with the knowledge we have obtained through our life experience (which, according to the author, is more important than gender, ethnicity, and other such demographic components in determining receptivity) to convince you that reading this book will make a major impact on your career. For instance, let's parse the twenty-one italicized words in the first line of this foreword. We know from our experience as authors that quotes such as the one contained in this foreword are used to sell a book. The publishers put such quotes—called blurbs—on the book cover to increase interest and sales. We want to imply an urgency to read the book, so the first word is "RUSH" in caps. The need to emphasize the name of the writer before the book is so that any previous credibility the writer has engendered will cause people familiar with his work to consider buying and reading the book in expectation of valuable information.

We want to tell you, the potential reader, what the payoff is for purchasing and using this book whether or not you are a lawyer or studying to become a lawyer. And so we tell the truth—that you can become a great, not merely a good attorney; and we also use texting parlance so that our appeal is to a cross-generation of potential readers. You, the reader, can actually achieve a specific goal of becoming a great lawyer; so we use the word *can* rather than the word *may*. *May* implies a mere possibility. But the use of the word *can* implies that the goal of becoming a great lawyer is within your reach…as long as you invest some time and effort to read, digest, and try out what you learn. If you are considering becoming a student of the law or are just fascinated by what makes lawyers tick, then this is the book that steps inside the process. And, of course, we finish our statement with an exclamation point to indicate that the tenor of our message is meant to be strong and emphatic; we believe in Paul and the important lessons to be learned in this book for lawyers and non-lawyers alike.

Paul Lisnek's skills are not limited to dealing with a jury, for he is more than a jury consultant, he is also a trial lawyer and student of persuasion and communication. He is actually more like an interpersonal relationship advisor (or, for the legal-minded, a trial consultant). The articles in this book collectively tell you how lawyers shape a case, from the big picture to the most minute of details, all to the goal of mastering the Art of Lawyering. Paul lays out the science of dealing with people in the framework of a living, breathing, morphing case. He warns lawyers about what they need to know. For instance, in the twenty-first century you must be able to deal with round-the-clock media if you are going to be successful in achieving the best result for your client. For the non-lawyer, if you are a fan of legal dramas or TV courtroom analysis programs like those on In Session (a channel where you will often find Paul and us appearing as commentators), then this is the kind of insight that will excite you and provide you with an insider's feel.

In our vocations as a trial attorney and a forensic pathologist, we work inside many a courtroom. While there are differences associated with all cases, the information Paul discloses in this book is priceless and constantly applicable. The chapters address the fundamental issues and situations that today's lawyers find themselves in: from crafting their case to taking effective depositions, seeking settlement through negotiation and alternative dispute resolution methods, and ultimately gearing up for trial and appeal when necessary, *The Art of Lawyering* reaches into every facet critical to legal practice. Furthermore, Paul's background in communication and as an ethics commissioner helps him tackle issues of professional responsibility, what it means to be an ethical and respectable lawyer, and even how to build business in a tough economy.

Like us, Paul lives much of his life in front of the television camera and at a radio microphone and he shares the secrets for handling the challenges of media inquiries, such as when a reporter's goal may be more to get a story or elicit a leak than to present the truth. Lawyers in the public eye must be careful where they tread!

On a personal note, we have known Paul and his family for years as a result of first meeting him in a professional setting. He is truly a terrific person and loyal friend…which is why we even named one of the characters in our book, *Skeleton Justice*, after him…in the form of a skilled prosecutor!

So we repeat, "RUSH to read Paul Lisnek's new book, *The Art of Lawyering*. If you do, you can become a great, *gr8* attorney!" Whether you are in the courtroom as lawyer, witness, juror, or consultant, this book is the on-point strategic manual you'll want to keep close at hand.

Linda Kenney Baden, Esq., and Michael Baden, M.D.
New York City, 2010

PART I.

LAWYERS ARE MADE, NOT BORN

THE ART OF LAWYERING AND CLIENT DEVELOPMENT

Becoming and Staying a Lawyer
High-Quality Service and Client Loyalty

The Art of Lawyering asks this question: is lawyering actually an art? I would think it is a skill, wouldn't you? The truth is, what a lawyer does requires a skill set that can be learned (at least to the extent that law school classes teach the skill set), but that's not what the art is intended to reference. Lots of people graduate from law school, pass the bar, and undertake the practice, but it is a fine few who truly get the artistic component to the skill base. The art refers, in many ways, to that which is beyond the rules, the cases, and the actual skills. It is about the insight, the gut, the feel, the voice, the gesture, the talent. Lawyering is indeed an art, for those who wish to excel, to stand out amid the crowd of lawyers, to be the go to lawyer for both clients and fellow lawyers.

It is with this concept in mind that I write with a hope that this book leads every lawyer to take pause, reflect on the values so important to the ethical and successful practice of law, and open his or her mind to the importance of the power of communication addressed on the pages that follow.

I begin with the beginning, a message to the new lawyer who is just joining this most noble of professions.

Follow the Yellow Brick Road

Five Essentials for the Young Lawyer

Welcome to the noble profession of the law! It is a fascinating journey, to be sure, upon which you are about to embark. With the many words and good wishes that have accompanied the pomp and circumstance of admission to the bar, it is now time to take a deep breath and recognize the great responsibility placed upon you as a lawyer. For the first time, perhaps, there is real risk that accompanies the decisions you will make, real lives and freedom that depend on your knowledge, your skills, and your judgments. Yes, the party's over now, but the fascinating journey of law is just beginning.

The metaphor of the yellow brick road is not a bad one when considering the importance of following the ethical and proper roads required in this land of laws. Stay on the road, and you are sure to encounter professionalism, satisfaction, and prosperity. Move off the road, and you confront forests of confusion, fields of risk, and uncertainty. It is far easier than you might imagine to stray off the path, so take a moment to consider the guidance suggested here. It is critical that you avoid the pitfalls and real-world problems that nearly always find their way to new practitioners who are just beginning their practice of law. By knowing and living by a few basic rules, your transition can be made a bit easier. Because you are well trained to understand lists (I am guessing you had a few hundred to study for your final exams and certainly for the bar exam), you should find the following to be user friendly. Here is the first such list for use in the real world:

1. It's a round world.

I learned this lesson early in my career when I allowed my desire to win at all costs to overtake my common sense. I actually was so intent on winning a motion for summary judgment and awarding of fees against the other side that I put any interpersonal relationship with that lawyer aside. You need to know now that you will meet and work with the very same lawyers over and over again through the years and throughout your entire career. As large as the legal field may be in your city (and yes, I am including Chicago, Los Angeles, and New York City), it is amazing how incredibly *small* it really is in practice. The judges will come to know you and get a sense of what motivates you and how ethical you are in your practice; other lawyers will quickly learn how you view the practice of law; and your clients will almost immediately sense whether they can faithfully place their trust in you.

Treat every judge, colleague attorney, and client with respect. Appreciate their points of view and the difficulties they encounter that may prevent them from meeting your deadlines and expectations each and every time. You will soon see that you need *their* understanding and often cooperation as well in a variety of matters. Work things out. The judge is a matter of last resort, not first resort. Judges would much prefer you to work in a civil manner with your colleagues and to know that you can rely on the court as a shield to protect justice, rather than a sword to demand it.

2. Clients don't grow on trees; they must be cultivated from the ground up.

I know far too many lawyers who believe that clients retain them strictly because of their legal skills and insights. Many lawyers seem to be a true legend in their own mind! This is not twenty-first-century thinking, at least from a client marketing perspective. These days, clients *assume* you are competent and a fine lawyer; they would not even agree to meet with you if you did not already have the requisite excellent level of skill they expect from the start. This expectation, however, is not why clients remain with their lawyers over time. Today, the stiff competition among lawyers is grounded in clients' expectations of *service* from their lawyers. In marketing, there is an old adage that says that it costs merely $1.00 to keep a client, but it costs $5.00 to find a new one (I'll bet inflation has bumped those numbers up quite a bit!). Point is, the cost of replacing a dissatisfied client is much higher than the cost of keeping current clients satisfied. You can't justify the price tag of wooing back a lost client or making extensive efforts to get a new client who does not believe you will provide the service quality they demand.

How do you keep the client-retention dollars small? Call your clients back as quickly as you can after they call you. Do not make them chase you; do not make them call you several times until they finally catch you at your desk; and do not otherwise make them wonder what is going on with their cases. Whether you represent sophisticated corporate executives or a defendant facing a prison term, every client has the right to reach and connect with his or her lawyer in a reasonable time. I will tell you that one of the main reasons clients report their lawyers to the state disciplinary commission or board is because they have been chasing that lawyer and can't get him or her to respond. Clients will not go away; they will report you…with a vengeance. I don't blame them.

Make it a practice early on in your career, from the first day, in fact, always to return every telephone call by the end of each business day. In addition, make it a practice to keep every client informed on a reasonably regular basis. This is the type of legal practice that leads clients to seek you out. It will also, candidly, place you light-years ahead of most of your colleagues. It's where client service is today, and the expectations ain't turning back!

3. Scout's motto: always be prepared.

I don't remember much from my scouting days, limited as they were, but I do remember the importance of always being prepared. And I do remember the teaching of my friend, the late and very great Johnny Cochran, who often talked of the three P's in a successful law practice: Prepare, Prepare, Prepare!

There may be no greater truth when it comes to courtroom presentations, settlement conferences, and legal drafting. You are trained to know the law, but you also need to give thought to the different styles, expectations, and demands a judge or client may make of you. Substantive knowledge alone will not be enough to produce success in a field that relies greatly on strategy, technique, and style. What makes the great lawyer is not the extent to which that lawyer knows the law (although that is a useful ingredient indeed), but rather it is the manner in which that lawyer relates to and with others. Take some time to understand the styles of others and work with their differences, not against them. You will find success in your relationships with others and ultimately will prosper in your casework as well.

4. Money makes the world go 'round.

While not a tribute to the spirituality that guides us in our practice (after all, didn't we all enter the practice because we wanted to bring justice to the world?), there is a certain concrete reality that clients must and fortunately will, for the most part, pay for the legal services you render. Certainly everyone knows this as a truth, but for some reason, it is the most uncomfortable of topics; lawyers hate having to discuss their fees. Maybe it's because we don't enjoy putting a price tag on services. I can say that my out-of-pocket expenses must be reimbursed, but having to say that my time can command a value of hundreds of dollars an hour? That's tough to do...unless you are worth it and truly believe you are worth it.

Clients need to know the financial expectations that are required if they are to receive your high-quality legal services. Be up-front with fees. Clients know they need to pay fees. If you are charging too high a fee, you won't have many clients and you'll lower your hourly rate accordingly. But when a client has no gripe with your $350-per-hour fee, you must be worth it, sometimes because you can accomplish in fifteen minutes what a less-expensive associate would take two hours to do. Ultimately, when clients hire a less-expensive associate, they end up paying more overall for the same project.

5. The world can go 'round without money.

While not required to perform service for the public good, lawyers experience no greater warmth or satisfaction from being in our profession than when helping those who are unable to help themselves. Make a personal commitment that you will help as many people as you can who cannot afford legal services but who have a right to access the legal process. No fee can match the satisfaction you will feel. Commit to starting with at least one case this year and increase that number each year as much as you are able. You won't regret it.

If it is so important, then why doesn't the American Bar Association require that we do *pro bono* work? The problem is a difficult one. Some lawyers have the resources and income to permit them to make the effort. Others experience tough times, and putting resources into *pro bono* work could force the lawyers to close shop. I encourage you to make as much an effort as your personal situation will allow you to do.

Finally, while law school and the bar exam are behind you (you are not dreaming; it's over!), understand that your education has only just begun. Law school brought you to the starting line; now you must rely on continuing-education courses, both substantive and practical, to enhance your knowledge and your skills as you begin your journey. Your style and your integrity, however, are components that are difficult to teach; they have to be innate.

Now go forward with the trust of your clients, the faith of the profession, and the knowledge that the answers to all your career concerns rest in asking questions and listening carefully to those who have been walking ahead of you. The greatest wealth of all is the rich legacy of experiences of the lawyers who have preceded you to the bar.

Go proudly in *their* footsteps knowing that *future* lawyers may very well look to *you* for guidance when they begin their own career. How rewarding that will be for you!

It is difficult if not impossible to forge ahead discussing the various skills that a lawyer needs to be successful without first addressing the 800-pound gorilla in the room. The heavy weight is the question that non-lawyers who pick up this book will likely be asking themselves under their breath while skimming the back cover: "Don't we have too many lawyers already? Aren't there too many lawsuits? Aren't verdicts out of control? Aren't lawyers the reason that insurance premiums and costs in general keep going up? And do lawyers have any ethics anyway?" Let's address the issues head-on.

First Thing We Do, Let's Kill All the Lawyers

Improving Public Perception of the Law

Talk about lawyers and ethics in the same sentence, and you can hear the laughter erupting among the crowd. "Lawyers and ethics; isn't that an oxymoron?" our well-meaning friends like to ask with a hearty chuckle. How upsetting this comment should be to us! Well, maybe, just maybe, most lawyers are indeed good, talented professionals whose aim is to assist their clients in resolving their problems. Maybe there is no such thing as a norm of unethical lawyers. That's where I come out on this issue, and having served as a disciplinary commissioner on the Attorney Registration and Disciplinary Commission in my home state of Illinois for well more than twenty years, I have good reason and strong support to back up my position.

Let me be honest with you. It drives me crazy when people complain that there are too many lawyers in this country, too many lawsuits filed, that all lawyers are unethical, and that life would be better for all if there were no attorneys in our society. The jokes may be funny and the sentiment may be real, but the truth is that these people just don't understand the critical role lawyers play in society. And I don't say this because I *am* a lawyer (that's both a disclaimer *and* a confession). I say it because it's true. These people don't get it, and I am not sure they ever have understood, as we see through the course of how lawyers were treated in history and even in the theater.

"First thing we do, let's kill all the lawyers." Remember that line from Shakespeare's *Henry VI, Part II*, spoken by the character Dick the Butcher? Written likely as a point of humor back then, it was not intended to say that lawyers were the problem of society but rather to make the point that if the bad guys wanted to take down the ruler and topple the government, the first thing they had to do was to kill all the lawyers. Regardless of Shakespeare's actual intent, though, it is clear that lawyers will forever have their characters maligned and purpose denigrated by non-lawyers (and playwrights, of course).

Laypeople like to point to surveys of public trust in which they can always count on lawyers coming in last, or certainly below the profession of the dreaded used-car dealer. Again, such studies trigger laughter in people, because non-lawyers love to hate lawyers. I find it interesting that while people do not like lawyers, surveys also suggest that people note one glaring exception to this negative view of lawyers, and that exception is that people tend to love their *own* lawyer, believing they have found the one and only respectable person in the profession.

I know a woman who loves to hate lawyers. She considers all lawyers to be ambulance chasers; nothing I ever say to her appears to adjust her viewpoint in a positive direction. But then she suffered an accident herself. She had been on a cruise ship and got bumped by another passenger on the ship, which led to her taking a fall and breaking her wrist. Well, this anti-lawyer, anti-lawsuit woman could not wait to sue the woman who bumped her, the ship, and the cruise line. She wanted to sue everybody and anybody who could compensate her for her injury. She interviewed with several lawyers, but none of them would take the case. Not one lawyer saw a viable legal theory to be applied against any of the suggested defendants. I would argue that this was the system working at its best. I assumed that this challenge to her opinions would finally help her see the light, that not all lawyers are case-chasers who file frivolous lawsuits.

Alas, her anger with lawyers *increased*, because the entire profession failed to see that she had the only worthwhile and important case ever to emerge in the history of humankind! Do you see a possible pattern here? Laypeople are often misinformed, biased in their views on the legal process, and so unfamiliar with exactly how the process works that the tendency is for them to view lawyers in a negative light without looking at the truth about how lawyers make and reach decisions.

I know, there is "that woman who got a jury to award her two million dollars for spilling some coffee on herself at McDonald's." Everyone knows that case, but does anyone know that an appellate court ultimately reduced that jury verdict award to a reasonable amount? Does anyone understand that sometimes jurors and judges make errors in judgment and corresponding awards, and that we have an appeals process to correct what would otherwise stand as an error? The corrections never seem to make the newspaper. The point is that lawyers have a job to do, which is to represent their clients with an appropriate and ethical zeal and within the boundaries of the law and the rules of professional responsibility. Mistakes occur in the system, and these should be addressed; but that's no reason to hang all lawyers out to dry.

In fact, rather than listening to people who wish to complain about Hollywood celebrities who get away with murder, I offer these vocal folks the following thought: yes, it may be true that some people are not convicted of a crime they may well have committed, but isn't it wonderful that we live under a legal system in which, even in the face of overwhelming evidence and a strong gut feeling that someone committed a particular offense, a prosecutor (the government) must prove guilt beyond a reasonable doubt, and if the government can't dot the i's and cross the t's that person gets to go home? In fact, is it not a more egregious error when a person who is *not guilty* of a crime is found guilty of that crime? Is it not worse for our society when a person is wrongfully accused and convicted of a crime, and then serves twenty-five years in jail, only to have DNA tests ultimately prove that the person did not commit that crime? If we're being honest, that's our system at its worst. That's when the system is truly broken, and the cost great. Our society is better served when a guilty person goes free because a jury has a reasonable doubt than to have a person convicted and serve time for a crime he or she did not commit. Give that some thought and see where you come out on the issue.

What do we do about the problem? If you are a lawyer reading this book, all you really need to do is educate others and not tolerate lawyer attacks. Be sure that people in your life understand, as best you can manage it, what lawyers *really* do, how we do it, and the fact that we are really fine people for the most part. If you are not a lawyer, however, then you are probably open to my message anyway, because I doubt you would have otherwise taken your valuable time to read this book written primarily for lawyers. I don't mean to offend any non-lawyer, but I have always thought that the reason people do not like lawyers is because, truth be told, people are intimidated by lawyers. They fear the skills, knowledge, and power that legal training provides, or perhaps more accurately, they fear the harm that can be imposed on the non-lawyer by one who understands and therefore can "manipulate" the legal system. How does one resolve such fear without comparable education and experience? Fair enough. Only lawyers get trained in the art of advocacy and the skill of forcefully representing the position of others beside themselves. This is a powerful set of skills indeed, but I would rather people be respectfully in awe of them than to fear, insult, or otherwise feel the need to disparage them and the lawyers who possess such training.

Now the above being said, it is true that lawyers have some work to do to gain the trust of the public. Ads on television that suggest lawyers are all about handling personal injury does not do justice to the expansive realm of legal services. Most legal services are not as consumer-appealing, so they are not the source of fascinating television or radio ads. People complain that lawyers charge high fees for services they do not understand. Lawyers don't produce widgets or commodities. It may be easier to put a price on the drafting of a will or contract, but how does one put a value on time and advice? I acknowledge this is difficult. But this means lawyers need clients to understand that legal expertise and insight has significant value; greater experience may very well mean more valuable insight. This is why lawyers charge more for their services the longer they are in practice.

The solution to the problem of how a more positive image of lawyers can be created rests in education. Do you not find that when people are educated and have significant exposure to life's experiences, they tend to be more open in their views and more accepting of those people who are different from themselves, and they just plain "get it?" Those with less education often fall prey to fear, innuendo, conjecture, or anything else they do not understand. For example, why is it that when a new lawyer show premieres on television and gains popularity, applications to law school almost always go up? It's because the mission, purpose, and lifestyle of these fictional lawyers we watch on television intrigue people. They often *like* the lawyers they see portrayed on TV, and believe that in fiction is the reality of a promising legal career for them, but like anything else, television is not a true reflection of reality.

The mission is to educate the uneducated and not tolerate the myriad of lawyer jokes and lawyer attacks that may cross your path. The jokes may be funny, and perhaps *not* laughing will make you appear a person of little humor, but if you use common sense, you can make the point. When you hear a lawyer joke, consider responding: "You know, I understand that lawyer jokes can be funny, but they really aren't fair. They don't represent what lawyers are all about and don't reflect all the good and important work that lawyers do both in and for our society." In other words, try to make a difference. Look, I am not equating lawyer attacks with the attacks some people make based on race, nationality, or gender, but it is interesting to note that as tolerance of difference grows in our society, jokes and attacks based on such categories are no longer in good taste and should not be tolerated. Wouldn't it be great if lawyer attacks were also found to be an inappropriate standard by which to judge the work and accomplishments of an entire profession? Wouldn't it be wonderful if society's dialogue focused on the *pro bono* efforts of lawyers and on the lawyers who work to represent the rights of those who are under-represented in our society and also on the improvements that have been made in the safety of consumer products that are the result of lawsuits? Imagine the positive consequences of our efforts to improve the image and reputation of the legal profession.

Once we are given our "tickets" to enter the practice of law, we are assumed to be ready to go. That is, once licensed, we can write a complex will, try a murder case, and depose an experienced economist. Nothing could be further from the truth. Law school's valiant effort to teach us to think like a lawyer fails to train us to practice law. The ready and able assumption permeates every level of a firm; it is my hope that every lawyer will give pause and consider the need to bridge the gap between theoretical education and practice and continue to train associates through the early years and thereafter.

Back to School

Continuing Education for Every Lawyer in the Firm

There is a truth being presupposed here. The assumed truth is that lawyers learn their craft through practice and training, yet whenever I read a survey or lawyer-on-the-street interview, it is apparent that our training comes from watching more senior lawyers (senior to ourselves, anyway) practice their skills. Somehow, if we watch others enough and model that behavior sufficiently, we'll magically become competent. For many lawyers this is a hope not strongly grounded in the realities of practice.

Consider for a moment the number of great trial lawyers you can name. Whether from history or a survey of currently well-respected trial lawyers, what do these great names have in common? The answer is simple, yet disconcerting: a level of credibility that reaches the power of charisma. They had or have a natural ability to relate to jurors with impact. Jurors not only believe the arguments being put forth by that lawyer, they go on to accept the suggested case outcome proposed by that lawyer, an outcome always favorable to the client, of course. Why is this disconcerting? Because I am not sure how to learn greatness.

There are a myriad of technique books in which the great lawyers share their secrets of success with those of us who wish that either we were these great lawyers or we could at least become great in our own right. We must keep in mind that the suggestions are just that, secrets to *their* success. It does not mean that each one of us cannot reach a level of high distinction in the profession and in the eye of the public. To the contrary, every new lawyer and veteran alike has within himself or herself the ability to become one of the finest lawyers ever. The answer lies in the extent and means by which we seek to develop our skills and abilities. I am drawing a distinction between attending albeit wonderful CLE programs that bring excellent speakers together who share important information (most often in the form of a talking-heads panel, which becomes a struggle for the sleepy among us), and the efforts expended to train ourselves to become better-skilled lawyers. It is here that arguments for mandatory education fall short as they relate to the trial lawyer. A meaningful program for the trial lawyer means a program that requires participation, individual skill building, and feedback on individual performance.

As a national CLE speaker myself, I am always gratified when trial lawyers in attendance at my programs are eager to pay attention and learn something from the day. I am equally dismayed when I meet those lawyers whose practice area has nothing to do with my topic, but they explain to me that continuing-education-reporting rules require them to get their hours in "by Friday," so for fear of losing their license they take whatever program is being offered because they otherwise will come up short on education hours. See the problem? They likely made no time in the year to seek out and sign up for programs that would really make a difference for them in practice; they likely believe that there is little for them to learn by attending a session and that their time is better spent drumming up new business rather than developing an existing skill base. The reality is that all lawyers have to take training and education seriously, see the value in it, and take programs with a potential for making them better lawyers.

It is true that what works to make some other lawyer great may not necessarily work to make us great. Technique and effect is a personal thing that each of us needs to develop in our own way. What is important is that each of us take the time to train, gain, and develop the skills of great lawyering. The lawyers who have a natural ability for courtroom success are blessed to be sure. They have an innate sense of people, especially jurors, and know what it takes to have others champion a cause (verdict) presented by them. Absent that internal sense, the vast majority of lawyers need to work hard to develop their skills.

Yet it astounds me to see the number of law firms and individual lawyers who have no time for training or choose to make no time for training beyond what is required by the mandatory education requirements of the state bar. There is too much work sitting on our desks, there are too many hours to bill (after all, bonuses depend on it), and there is even the question of how much credit our firm will give us for taking time to get trained in lawyering skills. Among the firms who *do* devote time to training, how much of that time is scheduled to occur on a weekend or other off-work time block because the regular workweek is too important to spend time investing in skill development? Think about it. What is the message of a firm that *encourages* skills training but never wants it to occur on firm time?

It's not for the lack of good intent or a commitment on the part of every lawyer to be the very best he or she can be. It's just about the degree to which we actually practice what we preach. For example, consider the value of an ongoing training program that year after year requires new and experienced lawyers alike to participate in a series of skill-developing efforts. Programs that include videotaping and critique, programs that rotate faculty so new perspectives are gained throughout the experience, and programs that bring in outside experts or teachers to assist in the skill-development efforts all represent a firm dedicated to making a difference in its lawyers' growth and success. Sometimes we forget that many of the law professors we respected in class are willing to assist private firms with the development of their new lawyers. Sure, the professors make money giving such training (I am guilty of it myself), but it is all about the investment in those on whom the firm will depend to continually provide excellence in work product and service.

I recognize that the main message of this section is directed at law firms where there are several lawyers to be trained and a presumed set of resources to pursue these efforts in-house. I do not mean to neglect the solo practitioners or very small firms among you who feel like skipping this section because for you training would be for one or only a few people, and the resources and time are even a greater challenge; after all, if *you* aren't billing time, there is *no* income getting generated. You are not exempt from this message though. Your clients similarly expect and need an attorney who is up to speed on current law, especially in those areas that are ever changing, and who knows the latest presentation technology and skills. The good news is that every state presents a myriad of program options at the state and local bar association level, and there are bar associations (the American Bar Association being the largest) that are forever presenting programs at modest fees and that can provide the same quality, albeit not with the direct focus that an in-house program brings. The point is that there is no excuse for any lawyer not to seek out the best programs, some substantive and some skill-based, to ensure overall growth and progress every year.

Training is a commitment that needs to be considered a paramount requirement for every lawyer. If your firm does have an existing training program, how often is it reviewed to ensure that it offers and provides the value it should provide to the lawyers? Does your specific department offer programs and speeches that it labels continuing legal education, but in reality get presented to audiences of only a few who actually make the time to attend them? Have you worked with an expert in education who understands what a well-rounded program requires to ensure that a specific law firm program works well? Does your firm management permit (or for that matter encourage or require) the lawyer participants to evaluate each program and offer suggestions for improvement?

If you have considered developing a lawyer training program, consider taking the following steps:

1. Hold a meeting of the firm leadership and agree that lawyer training is a non-negotiable component to client service, that the firm will do what is necessary to establish a valuable and meaningful program.

2. Consult with an educational expert who can assist in establishing the structure and design of the program.

3. Establish a well-thought-out curriculum that includes skill development and has follow-up components to ensure that the skills being taught are also being integrated into each lawyer's practice. There is little use in a one-day program whose message is appreciated but soon forgotten by the lawyers. Ensure follow-up and monitoring over time. This is time and effort well spent if we are going to train and, in effect, create effective lawyers for the future.

4. Ensure that the program occurs, at least partially, during the workweek, and in some way ensure that lawyers are given credit for training equal to the credit received for hourly billing, where appropriate. Otherwise, training becomes a burden placed second to the perceived and very real need of getting hours in. The dedication to making better lawyers has to start with firm leadership and cannot be questioned when the firm puts its money where its demands are, literally.

5. Create an advanced program, perhaps by hiring outside national or local experts to help in ongoing training of even experienced lawyers. Remember, we may have all picked up bad habits in the "lawyer see, lawyer do" approach over the years. It is worth the effort to sharpen our skills on an ongoing basis.

6. Evaluate each step of the program, ensuring you are

meeting lawyer needs. Listen to the feedback, and work to present a program that motivates all lawyers so they look forward to the next program.

Some might claim that in the competitive legal market of today it is costly to train a highly paid new lawyer who will only leave to join some other firm, or that we do not have the time to both train ourselves and complete our cases in an effective and timely manner. It is true that training is time consuming and expensive, both in time devoted and billing time lost; however, every lawyer's commitment to excellence in our representation of clients leaves no other respectable choice. Training needs to be seen as a necessary cost of doing business in which you keep some lawyers and perhaps lose others. In the long run, training is a cost of doing business that will produce the fruits of victory in litigation and satisfaction among clients.

Assembling a group of talented lawyers or working solo as a talented lawyer is no guarantee that business will walk through the door. If clients do walk in the door, there is no guarantee that they will stay. Lawyers practice law under a false assumption—that talent equals business. It is an important awakening to realize that clients don't give points for excellence; they expect it. There is more to rainmaking than first meets the eye. The following three articles address this issue.

Paving the Road to Your Door

Quality Service Is the Key to Continued Business

Quality is a matter of perception. In fact, a lawyer cannot manage the perception; she or he can only manage the client's perception. Providing quality in process requires the effort of the entire firm.

Lawyers need to recognize that clients seek a balance between the fees they pay for lawyer time and service and the value received from those services. In fact, they often cannot distinguish between the work-product quality of various law firms. Excellent lawyers produce excellent work product, but few of them have a strategy for providing quality in the service that needs to accompany the product.

Improvement in service quality is the key to survival and success among lawyers and law firms in the twenty-first century. It is the only means of remaining competitive among legal service providers.

Clients buy legal services for different reasons. Some are economic buyers who evaluate fees, prices, discounts, and rates; others are technical buyers who seek to meet a specific one-time need; still others rely on their personal or business relationships to initiate and continue legal ties. Regardless of the type of legal buyer, no client who is unwilling to buy can be sold legal services; clients buy for their own reasons.

Consider the typical lawyer-client lunch: forty-five minutes of small talk followed by five minutes inquiring about legal services and five minutes spent on a pitch for legal services with the hope that the "sale" will somehow magically close. It is a sadly unrealistic approach for today's marketplace, yet it is the modus operandi in a competitive legal market. The key to success is quality.

The road to quality includes the following:

Teamwork

Comprised of members at all law firm levels (partner, associate, paraprofessional, and support staff), the team operates under the guidance of a selected leader. The team plans and organizes the projects in accordance with the needs of the client, as determined by processing information gathered through interactions with the client. Tasks are delegated appropriately, and the team meets on a regular basis to monitor the client project. Consistent contact with the client is essential if the lawyers are to properly monitor the client's situation. The team should not operate under a set of assumptions of what it thinks the client needs or wants. Regular interviews create the requisite sense of certainty.

Understanding the Client

Lawyers must know as much as they can about the client and the client's business (assuming, of course, it is a corporate entity). Regular visits with major clients ensure constant and updated information on that client's development. "I want or need more legal business" isn't the best reason for a meeting. A better approach to establish a viable and promising relationship would be something like this: "There have been some changes in the tax laws that can affect the way in which your company is managing its relationships and accounts. Let's get together and go through them so we can ensure you are protected against these modifications." By the way, such meetings to develop relationships are best conducted at no cost to the client. In an era of lawyer bashing (will this era ever end?), demonstrating actual concern for our clients goes a long way in client development and retention.

Client interviews should gather information about the company, its employees, the environment and market in which the company exists, the manner in which the company operates, and plans and directions for the future. We should monitor not only factual information related by the client, but also the client's feelings about his or her situation and needs.

Added Value

A successful quality-service strategy must focus on the client's needs and wants. It must address the client's agenda, not the lawyer's. Added value in client service comes not from assumptions about what the client expects or needs, but from continued interaction with the client. Sounds simple, but this principle is more difficult than it may first appear. Often we allow what we would want for our own business to define the advice we give to our clients; this is not the point. We can't properly evaluate our advice to our clients outside an understanding of *their* goals and values.

Service Strategy for Commitment

Every important client has a strategy developed that is client specific. It needs to be perceived as beneficial from the client's perspective. Moreover, the lawyer must be certain she or he can deliver the service and work product promised, within whatever time frame is promised. Plans also must include an implementation schedule. Finally, the plan must be carried out.

Keep in mind that clients have options not only in their business decisions, but also in their legal hiring decisions. They can select another lawyer or law firm if they are not satisfied with you. Ultimately, success in providing high-quality service to clients requires a commitment at every level from the lawyer and every member of the law firm. Everyone in the firm must deliver quality, from the senior partner to the most junior support person. Achieving this ideal often requires everyone in the firm to undergo training both in requisite skills and in the meaning of quality.

Simply put, lawyers must deliver the work product and service that clients demand today if they are to ensure that those clients remain with the firm in the future.

The Billing Game: You Can't Win If You Don't Play

Keeping Fee Terms Clear

The dreaded legal fee; for some reason, there is no subject as uncomfortable for a lawyer to discuss as the fee to be charged for services. One doesn't need to look far beyond the complaints made to a state's disciplinary authority to see that lawyers and their clients often do not see eye to eye on fees to be paid for legal services rendered. There seems to be a never-ending confusion about the nature and types of legal fees available, as well as the reasons clients do not pay all the fees that we lawyers bill.

First, the seemingly simplest rule of all must be set out and affirmed: discuss fees with every client.

The discomfort lawyers feel in discussing fees likely lies in the fact that we are not trained in the business aspects of the law in law school. We graduate, get our law license, and instantly we find ourselves having to discuss fees and actually calculate and state a value for our services. It is not easy to tell a client how much we think our time is worth. It would be much easier to sell a tangible thing of some sort, but the notion that all lawyers have to sell is *time*, well, that's much too esoteric to grasp, so we don't discuss it, and then the client is shocked when costs far exceed expectations.

Fees need to be discussed explicitly. If doing so creates discomfort, set them out by tying them to a particular service and not to the lawyer's value of time. For example, it is easier to say, "The firm charges $400 for a closing," than it is to say, "I charge $100 per hour, and I foresee four hours of my time for this project." A written fee schedule, including hourly rates, can be printed out and given to each client as a part of the discussion of legal services.

In this way, unexpected costs that cannot be avoided, costs that may arise in the form of complications to an otherwise standard project, won't come as a shock to the client. The lawyer will feel justified in charging the additional fees, but the client will likely feel ripped off by a bill larger than expected, unless the client knows the fee schedule.

Once fees are discussed or otherwise set out for the client, be sure to confirm the legal arrangement in writing and have the client sign an agreement on fee structure. This agreement will be essential should a fee dispute arise in the future between lawyer and client, pitting one person's word against the other's. By the way, any ambiguity in an agreement is going to be construed against the drafter, and that would be the lawyer, so avoid all this hassle by setting the arrangement out in writing and getting it signed.

As work progresses, be certain to forward detailed invoices to the client regularly. The invoice should include details of the work performed, the lawyer or assistant performing the work, and the rate for that service. These invoices provide the client with a device against which his or her overall legal budget can be monitored. Such an arrangement is a good idea even in contingency cases as a means of tracking the time put into a particular matter. For lawyers who increase their percentage at trial or on appeal, an ongoing record of the many hours expended makes larger fees more palatable for the client.

Why do clients refuse to pay bills for legal services? While there are many reasons, here are a few of the major ones:

- The bill is perceived to be larger than the lawyer led the client to expect.
- The bill is larger than the client was told it would be.
- The fees are set out in generic form without explanation or description, which leads clients to think that they are being ripped off by fees that seem to appear without grounding, explanation, or foundation.
- The bill is incomprehensible (long, detailed, and unclear).
- The bill includes every nitpicky detail (postage, actual telephone charges, copies), which seem small in an otherwise large fee case.
- Actual arithmetic mistakes lead to an overcharge.

The bottom line: when a client does not sense the value for services rendered, the lawyer can anticipate a complaint from that client.

The lawyer bill that *will* be paid will be sent to the client promptly, with sufficient detail, and will be reflective of the amount of work put into the project. Once again, when time is the commodity being sold, the scale of fairness and equity must be weighed against the client's perception of value, not the lawyer's.

Today's market is competitive indeed. Lawyers have to compete for business more than ever before, and those who have participated in legal beauty contests (where several law firms make formal presentations in an attempt to get awarded a client's business) know that lawyers are caught in a buyer's market.

It is no longer sufficient to be a great lawyer. Today, clients expect and assume that the lawyer and law firm will produce excellent work product; that's a given. What they also expect is excellent *service*, and they want to perceive significant value for the dollars they spend, especially because what they are buying is time. Part of this process is the exploration of alternative billing methods.

Lawyers need to recognize that in today's legal climate we can be creative in how we charge, rather than simply billing by hourly rates and contingency fees. I would argue, in fact, that competition requires creativity in billing.

Consider the following: project-based billing, in which the client is charged a set amount for a project regardless of the time expended to get it done correctly. Real estate closings and uncontested divorces are examples. Such an arrangement can be offered as an option to a fee cap, where the latter has a larger fee but provides the client with a choice of value.

For example, an initial public offering can be handled for a flat fee of $175,000 or for a fee cap of $200,000. The former gives the lawyer incentive to work efficiently, while the latter presents the possibility for the project to be completed at less than the project fee, but in any case not exceeding the defined cap.

Another alternative arrangement is the blended rate. A blended fee means that the senior lawyer's rate ($300 per hour), the associate lawyer's rate ($150), and so forth are all offered at a blended single rate, perhaps $215. It means that the client pays one rate regardless of service, and it is up to the law firm to have the work completed in the most efficient and effective manner possible. Project blending may be offered when a set fee or rate is given for the handling of one matter, so long as another known or future matter will also be given to the firm. In addition, discounts can be given, or at least offered, for various factors, including negative results.

In short, the type of billing arrangement offered to a client is limited only by the creativity of the parties, and, of course, by any applicable provisions of the jurisdiction's Rules of Professional Conduct.

Once you consider the range of possibilities, it is easy to see why straight hourly billing is no longer a desirable arrangement from the client's point of view. From the client's perspective, and fueled by the real presence of competition among law firms, there is too much room for negotiation for one to need to accept an old-world arrangement.

There is a good side to all of this flexibility in billing and fee arrangements. It means that the discomfort lawyers feel when setting out a fee structure can be more easily addressed by simply opening up about the topic of fees, putting it on the table, and then exploring client needs and even preferences for how that client wishes to be billed. Look, it's important that clients believe that their lawyer believes in them! Talking about fees and the work to be done to earn them is a good means of helping to establish that bond and keep the fee issue clear as well. New and novel fee structures can also lead to confusion, and should a client complain, you will want to be able to clarify how you arrived at the numbers billed.

In the world of getting new legal business, it's not only how you play the game, it's also the recognition and resignation to the fact that you'd best be willing to play the *billing* game. It's a buyer's market, and only the players willing to play on the client's turf and terms can win.

Convincing Clients You're Worth It

Achieving Client Loyalty

T hese days many law firms find themselves in the position of Shim, Mertz, and Matthews, whose senior partner, Haskell Luckpit, remarked, "These young lions all seem to be the same. They have no apparent idea or interest in what it might take to build a practice. They arrive fresh from school, grab the office, and then show up to put their feet on that desk, waiting for the clients to come through the door like they do on *Boston Legal*. They don't seem to recall that someone had to build this practice, just like any other business."

While lawyers may not have had to consider building their practice as an essential part of the business in days gone by, the current and foreseeable climate for the profession makes a workable development plan a must. Short of advertising, which carries a price in its implication for returns, there are many approaches to building and maintaining a strong client base.

The most effective approaches to building and maintaining a strong client base have one thing in common: a focus on the client, the client's perspectives, and the client's needs. This approach is a far cry from maintaining a focus on the attorney, the firm, or past success.

The days of wooing clients with two-hour lunches replete with martinis and fine food are over—not that we don't host such lunches; we do and we enjoy them, but they don't work as marketing devices anymore, just as drinking fiestas! Today clients find themselves in a buyer's market. They expect that the work product of any lawyer who seeks their business will be excellent. The argument that a lawyer is entitled to business because he or she wins cases or is an excellent lawyer doesn't hold weight anymore.

As frustrating as it is to accept, clients only hire excellent lawyers, so there must be something else that leads them to buy from a particular lawyer. In a nutshell, the answer must lie in the area of service. Lawyers must offer clients something beyond work product. Clients demand immediate attention, responsiveness, and excellent communication from their lawyer, all in addition to fine work product.

Several years ago, in the field of advertising, two wunder-kinder named Trout and Rees came up with a campaign that sold their client's services across the globe as "second best." The client was Avis car rentals, the slogan was "We're number two, so we try hard harder," and their success is advertising history.

Their book, *Positioning*, has some age spots on it by now, but it nevertheless offers an approach that contains the key attitude for any lawyer working at increasing referrals and improving relations with current and, especially, potential clients. They declared that a business's people, its organization, and the quality of its products or services mean absolutely nothing, inherently. The only value for all those things is the perception of their people, business, products, and services in the minds of their potential consumers. People will determine for themselves the value of the position your law firm will hold in their heads, totally apart from any objective value that might be placed on it.

Trout and Rees also speak to the competition created by established businesses and their position in the market overall. Using examples of businesses whose products or services were first to the market (Hertz, Kleenex, Crayola, Xerox, etc.), the authors contend convincingly that an established number-one position in the minds of the consuming public cannot be taken away by a competitor. That competitor can position itself favorably in relation to the old number one and hope, as in the case of Avis, that the public responds well to that positioning in their own perceptions.

The authors go on to warn the established and complacent firms that while the top spot may be protected from direct assault by, and loss to, the competition, they can most certainly lose their number-one positions on their own, through damage to the image that current and future clients hold in their minds. Again, the perceptions and the perspective of the clients, not the firm, are foremost. Similarly, in the law, other firms and lawyers may hold prominence in the minds of consumers, but it doesn't mean the veil cannot be pierced and the market opened to others.

What forms the position of your firm in the minds of those who would refer clients to you or in the minds of current and future clients themselves? More than anything else, it is human contact and interaction. According to studies conducted in retail businesses, where clients receive material products (unavailable to a service industry like the law), more than 80% of customers say they leave a business not because of traditional, business-related reasons, such as buying from competitors or relocation, but strictly because those customers' perception of the people, or usually one person who works for that business, has declined.[1]

Whether describing their contacts with these employees as exemplary of bad encounters, indifference, rudeness, or lack of service, the negative impression of usually just one individual's interaction was sufficient to drive away more than 80% of the customers who left those businesses. Market research has consistently shown over the years what has become a standard observation among marketing professions: A customer who likes your service will tell on average four of his friends, but if he dislikes your service, he will tell on average ten of his friends.[2]

Just to keep even in your clients' perceptions, your firm will need an average of 2.5 satisfied customers for every one who is dissatisfied. Remember, perceptions are subjective. The reality in your clients' minds is the one that counts. You may never

---

1 "Why a Customer Leaves." (Taylor's Bookstores, 1989).
2 "Word of Mouth in the Market." (Honeywell Corp., 1981).

have the opportunity to argue directly on behalf of your firm and its work, once the position you hold in a potential client's mind has turned sour. For the lawyer, it means a focus on client perceptions of the lawyers' work product and service quality.

Clients are not interested in the lawyer's talk about quality in service and work product; they demand to see it. For example, the time it takes for a lawyer to return a telephone call to that client and other forms of responsiveness are essential to client attitude and satisfaction level. Clients today expect lawyer willingness to customize billing formats, to provide case updates and other communication components, and to be open to talking about and negotiating almost every other facet of a matter.

Without these service factors, it should be anticipated that a client's business will go elsewhere. In a contest between a client's perceived reality and objective reality there is no contest; perception always prevails.

Fortunately, many of the perspective-building efforts necessary for success in practice development can be labeled common sense. Skilled and polite telephone handling, letters and calls returned promptly, meaningful contact with clients and referral sources, courtesy, humor, and recognition of each person's individuality beyond the limited frame of current business all can and will do wonders. After all, one of the catch phrases of this decade is "client retention," which can be the most valuable form of practice development.[3]

---

3 This article is based on Paul M. Lisnek and Eric Oliver's *Courtroom Power: Communication Strategies for Trial Lawyers.* (PESI LAW Publications, 2001).

"Thank You for Calling"

Managing the First Contact with the Lawyer

"Good day, the Law Offices of Mertz, Maude, and Matthews; how many I direct your call?" With this or some similar greeting, the firm's receptionist meets every client, lawyer, or judge. With these words, your firm's image, tone, atmosphere, and even quality are established. The absence of courtesy and interest in the voice of your firm's receptionist (and by the way, anyone who answers the telephone is, by definition, the receptionist for the firm) will almost guarantee a poor image and lead to a negative reputation, so this point also goes for the lawyer who answers the firm's telephone after hours.

For some reason, many lawyers have little difficulty informing a caller that they are a lawyer and are burdened by having to take a message for another lawyer. ("Oh, wait a minute; I'll have to get a pen," or, "Can't you just call back tomorrow?") Callers to a law firm expect politeness and service, regardless of the time they happen to call and no matter who answers the phone.

It doesn't seem plausible that a simple phrase or greeting can have such a major impact on a caller, but it most certainly does. Consider the residual effect of a reception that includes the voice of one who sounds too busy to provide attention to the caller or so uninterested that the caller is made to feel like a burden to the firm. In such cases, the first call to a firm can be the *last* call to that firm if the caller (which could be a potential client!) loses any desire to carry on a conversation.

The realities of risk in a telephone greeting are clear enough. Calls to law offices are often made by people with a problem, and because they have a problem, the callers can often be emotional, scared, angry, or anxious. The last thing they need (or may tolerate) is a greeting that is anything but inviting and warm.

Anyone answering the telephone who fails to exhibit politeness and professionalism to a caller sends a negative message and creates an unfavorable opinion of that firm. To avoid the concerns I raise here, some lawyers say, "We'll just let callers be greeted by a computer-generated voice." Nothing could be further from resolving the issue.

The goal of such computer technology is to replace the human voice with an automated response system that seeks to direct calls with the push of a button and the absence of personal contact. This technology can create several possible impressions, which cover a broad range: "This is really a state-of-the-art law firm that has devoted its resources to modernization," to, "This firm has dehumanized the client relationship to the outer limit, reflecting its lack of concern for and interest in its client."

When using computerization, it is essential that callers not get lost in the telephone maze. Is there anything more frustrating than computer directions that do nothing more than send you to additional non-human computer message buckets and ultimately into the lawyer's voice mail? It is truly possible in such a system never to reach a human voice, or worse yet, not to be able to exit the system with the simple push of a button to reach a live voice at any point. The latter is critical to any computer-generated system; let callers know that they may leave computer hell simply and at any time they choose to do so.

Every computerized voice system needs a "human out." At any point, there should be an option that permits the caller to reach a human being, which would include a direct dial to the lawyer's office that is picked up by voice mail. Always give the caller an option to leave a message or to transfer out of the system to an assistant or receptionist.

In addition, voice mail messages should be updated daily to inform the caller whether you are in the office but temporarily unavailable, out of the office and will return shortly, or unavailable for the day. Clients and other callers can accept a lawyer who is not available when they call; they just want to know when they can expect to have their call returned. This expectation is fair enough in a highly competitive profession where we not only need to work for the business but also must provide top service to maintain and keep it.

Once the call is picked up, remember that clients, like all people, greatly resent being made to wait on hold for an attorney to finally pick up the phone. If the attorney cannot immediately accept the call, then the receptionist should be instructed to take a message and assure callers when they can be expect for the call to be returned. A specific time at which the call will be returned puts the caller at ease and puts an end to an otherwise endless round robin of messages. And oh, yes, you must actually return that call at the designated or promised time.

Simply put, all telephone calls should be returned on the same day, and an inability to return the call personally within that time should be eased with a telephone call from a secretary or other assistant who can find out how that caller can otherwise be assisted. There is little question that diligent return contact with callers is an unfortunately well-kept secret to lawyering success.

Here are a few rules for effective telephone reception. As you review these (and, I hope, share them with anyone who answers the phone in your firm), consider how many of these rules are violated each time you make a call to another office or company.

- Always begin the call with a greeting of "Good morning," "Good afternoon," "Good evening," or "Good day." Even if your day is less than good, there is no reason to impose negativity on the firm's callers. They have sufficient problems of their own that they don't need to be greeted by someone who may also be having a bad day.

- Do not sound hurried, rushed, or burdened by the telephone call, regardless of how hurried, rushed, or burdened you may be at that time. Callers have their own agenda, concerns, and goals. They do not care that the receptionist is very busy at the time they answer the call. To callers, their call *is* the priority.

- Do not chew or crunch into the telephone while answering. Even the unexpected call can wait an extra ring for food to be swallowed before the call is answered professionally by someone with newly focused attention.

- Ask "How may I direct your call?" rather than assuming callers want to speak to a particular lawyer. In many cases, a caller's questions can be answered better by a paralegal, scheduler, or accountant. Find out what the callers are after and save everyone time by sending them to the proper place. Having said that, do not direct a call away from the lawyer requested just because you think that someone else can better handle the call. The reality is that clients often think that only the lawyer can answer their call, and even if they are wrong, "no good deed goes unpunished" comes into play when they get angry that someone has chosen to redirect their call. That move can be interpreted as insulting.

- Assuming you have answered and already said, "Please hold," do not keep callers on hold for more than a few seconds without checking to see if they can continue to wait or prefer a return call. The request should be, "Can you hold?" and wait for the answer. If the response is, "I really can't," then the call should be taken at that moment and not met with a shift to the hold position before the answer ever got heard.

- Call every caller back on the same day he or she calls you. This is the secret to good client and colleague relations.

Amazingly, most client relationship problems can be resolved or appeased with the simple respect shown by how a telephone call is handled. View the six simple rules above as the ingredients to an almost certain guarantee of satisfied clients and increased congeniality among lawyers and others when they are trying to reach you.

Try it; you'll like it, and so will they.

PART II.

COMING TO TERMS

LAWYER AS NEGOTIATOR AND MEDIATOR

Negotiating Compensation
Finalizing Terms
Mediation and Arbitration

"Can I Have a Raise?"

Negotiation: The Psychological Process

The lines have been drawn forever: As my annual salary review approaches, I take in a deep breath and repeat over and over in my head that I know I am worth far more than I am being paid.

Except when I get into the meeting with my supervisor, I hear (in a fairly firm and gruff tone), "You are not worth half of what we are *already* paying you, and your current salary is far more than it should be anyway, so I certainly hope you are not anticipating a substantial raise."

Am I really not worth my salary? Am I being underpaid? Overpaid? Are we on different planets? How can I know?

These are actually trick questions.

This article seeks to provide insight on the process of negotiating salary and benefits. The theory that underlies the process is, of course, applicable in most other negotiations as well, so if salary negotiation is not a concern for you, read on with an eye toward the parallels to case settlement, the purchase of a home or car, and more personal negotiations with family members. The concepts work; it's just the setting that changes.

No one can ever know how much someone is worth, and we will never be able to determine the right number in any objective sense. We certainly try. We conduct and read comparative studies made among others around the city in our similar capacity. We look around the state and country for indicators. The statistics are certainly available all over the Internet (isn't Google an amazing thing?) if you want to know how much people are paid in a particular job at a particular level of experience. But then again, it's easy enough to draw distinctions. "Well, you didn't go to as fine a school as the people in that survey." "Hey, we're not made of money like the people in those studies."

The point is that negotiation is a psychological process. There is little objective sense in much of it, but we do our best to create it by calculating how much money we need to live on and pay our regular bills, how much more will get those outstanding loans down, how much more will provide a reasonable standard of living, and how much more will provide our family with a fair standard of living. We put pencil to paper with these numbers and create a working level of information from which to approach the negotiation.

Is it really about *money*? After all, I pick up the paper and read about another young associate who has killed himself by jumping out of the window on the twenty-second floor, and when his family sues the firm over unreasonable work hours, the court finds there is no cause of action because there is no such thing as unreasonable work hours when you practice law "in the big city." (That's a real case, you know.) Now I begin to question the non-monetary factors, like the quality of life and the fact that I would like to live a long one. And what about health benefits, vacation time, and flexible workdays? Are these intangibles worth more than the *money*? Would I be willing to give up something related to one of these factors to gain something on one of the others? Would the firm be more willing to give me some of these non-monetary in lieu of more money? Does our employer consider these factors? Does he or she really care about these issues? Is this negotiation a slam dunk, (no reference to former CIA Director George Tenet intended!) meaning I will be told what my new salary is and I have no input in this process; I simply sit and listen to a soliloquy with no invitation to dialogue? Will I look wishy-washy or lose out on more money unnecessarily because I bring up these factors? And can my employer really understand my situation?

The employer has his or her own factors to consider, as well. Do we have more people employed here than we really need, given the current economic situation? Does the future look bright in terms of growth and income, or are there clouds along the horizon? Is the employer's quality of life not so great itself, so there is really no burning desire to ensure that yours is any better? Does the employer consider you a valuable asset, not easily replaced in a world where most people are perceived to be, candidly, fungible? Do we really know the answers to these questions as we enter the salary review session? And if our employer does provide some indication as to the answers to these questions, do we believe he or she is telling the truth? After all, isn't life just full of posturing?

As we enter the salary negotiations, the butterflies in our stomachs begin to make more sense. We don't have a clue to the answers to the questions we have about the other person's situation. In fact, we can't be certain that the information being related to us is even true.

With all our efforts to make it an objective, concrete process, negotiation is really a process of trying to find out what is going on inside someone else's head and to find a way to strategically relate to the other person what is going on inside our own head. Once you recognize and accept this, you are ready to become a better negotiator.

Here's what we know: A *successful* negotiation is one in which both parties leave the process *believing* that they have done well. If I get more money than I was expecting, I am satisfied. I may never know that you were willing to pay me still more money, but negotiated me down. Does it matter, so long as both parties are happy?

An example: you want to buy a used car from someone whose ad you see in the newspaper. You are prepared to pay $5,500 for the car and intend to start with a lowball offer of $3,850 and go from there, but upon opening with your offer, the seller says, "Sold!" How do you feel? You just got the deal of the century, didn't you? You saved $1,650 off of what you were willing to spend, but you're probably sick to your stomach, because your offer got accepted *too quickly*. You are now convinced that something is wrong with that car and that it isn't worth the $3,850 you have to pay. Truth be told, it really may be the deal of the century! Maybe the seller just needs some cash fast, heard an acceptable number, and was willing to call it a success. Nevertheless, the seller would have been better served to provide a counteroffer.

The fact is that you'd feel a lot better being forced to pay something *more* than $3,850 and right up to $5,500. How can that be? Again, it is the psychological nature of the process, the give and take that has to occur for the parties to feel as though they are working toward an acceptable deal. The questions raised are interesting: is it true that the buyer feels bad with the first offer being quickly accepted? Yes. Is it true that a haggling between buyer and seller would lead to a happier, albeit higher result? True. And the most amazing question: does our buyer actually feel better if he or she were to pay *more* for the car through haggling than had it been purchased on the first offer? Once again, a resounding *Yes*! The message: you can't avoid the process and are better advised to understand and play within it.

Negotiation is the meeting of perceptions. Research conducted by a litigation consulting group called Trial Behavior Consulting Inc. indicates a shift over time in employee perception about compensation. The importance of compensation to law firm associates relates to their length of time in practice. When first joining a law firm, compensation does not emerge as a first-tier issue. Prestige, the nature of work done, and personalities of the firm members emerged as higher priority factors.

Over time, compensation increases in importance and integrates with firm profitability, partnership opportunity, and length of partnership track. Balancing this information is the finding that more than 50% of associates surveyed were *not* committed to longevity or partnership with their firm. It's easy to understand, isn't it, the statistics we see regarding the high rate of lawyer turnover?

Negotiating salary is, by its nature, a stressful situation. For some, the stress rests in a rational, logical determination of worth; for others it is an emotional process related to self-esteem and a sense of personal worth. Isn't our self-concept, integrity, and future all put on the line in this process? Moreover, the decisions made regarding our personal evaluation often have impact extending to co-workers and, through studies, to similarly situated people in other firms.

Success in this psychological process comes from being able to control the gathering and release of information between the parties to the negotiation.

Controlling the Talk: One Tough Job

Information Control in Negotiation

W e're interested in hiring you, Attorney Cianci. How much do you need for salary?"

Cianci ponders the offer from the prestigious law firm of Mertz, Maude, and Matthews, shifts in her seat, and wonders what the proper number should be. She decides to go a bit higher than she might expect, thereby permitting herself to lower the number if she needs to do so.

"Well, uh, I would like about $33,000, if that's all right."

"You got it," the hiring partner replies, and the deal is done. Why does Reese feel underpaid, then? If you remember that negotiation is a psychological process, it becomes quite clear that the offer and acceptance took place much too quickly.

The essential factor here is information control. In negotiation, like most other exercises, information is clearly power. Disclose your position, and you transfer a degree of power to the other side; gather information from the other side, and you gain some degree of power, because you know where the other side stands on a particular issue. You can then decide whether to move toward that party or implement some strategy to get the other party to see your side. This plan assumes, of course, that the information being disclosed is cloaked in some region of truth.

Seemingly a simple principle, the power to control the disclosure of information is an extremely difficult skill to implement. The reality is that it is human nature to disclose when we are asked a question. Rarely will we say, "I don't know," or, "I don't have an answer," even when we aren't certain of the answer. It feels much better to set out our demands, clarify our own position, and be sure others are hearing us, rather than sit back and make every effort to gather and probe the position of the other side.

Power rests in gathering and listening, not in talking and demanding. In negotiation, there is no factor more important than the ability to control what is disclosed to the other party; thus, when Cianci is asked for her desired salary, she feels the pressure to disclose some number. She isn't certain whether she is a cut above or below the employer's line, but Cianci feels she must say something. The secret, and it goes against human nature, is not to disclose a number, but to turn the interaction back to the hiring lawyer.

Consider what the firm may have been willing to pay for someone of Cianci's experience and background, perhaps $40,000 or more. Cianci will never know, because her first request was accepted. Once she states $33,000, can she really expect the hiring lawyer to respond, "Hey, it's your lucky day. We have $45,000 allotted to that position, and we would like to give it all to you."

In fact, because most negotiators proceed with a sense of wanting to do as well as possible for themselves, we can expect the employer to try to hire Cianci for *less* than her requested salary; it's just good business. Conversely, if the position paid well below Cianci's number, she can expect to be told she is out of the ballpark and should probably look elsewhere. This could even cut off her chance to explore exactly what the actual number might be and save face if she chose to accept a much lower number.

Cianci should in some fashion shift the question back. For example, "Well, Mr. Dukanytch, what did the firm plan to pay for this position?" This inquiry shifts the burden back on the employer to say, "We were looking for someone in the $40,000 to $45,000 range." Now Cianci is in the power position.

While she might say that she would have been happy with a much lower salary, the much more likely response is her acceptance of the $45,000 and an effort to increase the offer up a few thousand. Since negotiation is psychological, the employer would not be surprised by the request and likely has the authority to make an offer at a slightly higher level.

How likely is it that Dukanytch will provide a number for the salary, as opposed to first responding with an answer akin to "I asked you first"? Most people will respond to the request being shifted back to them. It's a fair enough tactic, and asked in a sincere and cooperative manner, it can be heard as an effort to move the process forward. If both players know the game, then Cianci can expect Dukanytch to shift it back again with a response along the lines of "Well, we can be a bit flexible, and it would really assist me in knowing what you need."

There is a difference between the levels of "need" and "want" in negotiation. As a rule, we will be unable to settle for a package that fails to meet our fundamental needs. We can, however, come to terms if our needs are met, even though we haven't added much icing to our cake, so the efforts to gain disclosure go back and forth. Someone will eventually put a number on the table, so the interviewee can listen for clues or indicators. If Dukanytch is consistent in seeking what Cianci "needs," this is clearly a search at the most basic level of negotiation. If the conversation proceeds at a level of "want," the message is far more flexible and acknowledges a salary level beyond survival. Thus, in the best of worlds, you can work to shift the inquiry on salary back to the interviewer, seeking the power that gathering information provides. If the inquiry is shifted back, you can at least listen for clues that indicate at what level the interviewer's sights seem to be set and trigger caution at stating a number or range that is outside reality.

Listening to the intent of the other negotiator provides significant information and therefore power.

For example, the use of a range in stating a position means little, except that it serves to establish a psychological floor or ceiling. When buyers (interviewers) set out a range, they know that the higher number becomes the starting point. "We wish to pay $40,000 to $45,000." Who will take the $40,000 and ask the employer to keep the rest? Sellers (interviewees) know that the lower number becomes the starting point: "I was hoping to be paid $40,000 to $45,000." Is there an employer who grabs the higher number?

Why use ranges at all? Why not just say, "We're offering $40,000" or "I want $45,000." We use ranges for two reasons. First, ranges suggest fairness and equity in position, and second, the final number is more likely to be closer to the spectrum's end point than a single number stated as "somewhere around $40,000." In another context, if the seller of a used car says, "I want $1,000 to $1,200," the selling price is more likely to be closer to $1,000 than if the seller says, "I want somewhere around $1,000." The car in the first instance will likely sell for between $900 and $950, while the other price range would probably trigger expectations in the buyer that the sales price is closer to $750. I find it interesting in my public seminars on this topic, to both bar associations and corporate audiences, for that matter, that audience members confirm this point through an in-class exercise almost every time.

When you are next asked for a desired salary, respond by shifting the inquiry back to the employer in a sincere search based on your own stated flexibility in position. Don't be surprised if you are offered a higher salary than you might have originally expected. Clearly there is more to the important skill of information control. The flip side to this skill is the *testing* of the other negotiator's position. While information is power, it is also true that we need to have a sense of validity of that information if our power is to increase realistically.

Reach Below the Surface to Find What Drives Someone

The Two Levels of Communication

Chris Matthews, host of MSNBC's *Hardball* has long intrigued me in the way he can stir great discomfort in his guests. Whenever someone states a strong position, Chris stares, raises his voice, and pointedly asks, "Why?" With that one word, guests stumble and bumble their way to a confused answer. In effect, Matthews has asked the other person to state the reasons that underlie his or her position. It is amazing how few people are prepared to address this underlying inquiry. In the world of salary and benefits negotiation, the ability to uncover the real meaning behind a position is critical to the process. To explain, let's step inside the law firm of Mertz, Maude, and Matthews.

Attorney Haskell asks his employer for an additional week of vacation, or perhaps another thousand dollars of salary. Rather than arguing over the term itself, the skilled negotiator wants to reach beneath the surface to uncover the true needs of the other person. To better understand this concept, it is necessary to understand the two levels at which we communicate.

The first level of communication is a behavioral or position level. This is where we state the specifics of what we want; for example, more money, better benefits, or whatever the terms of concern. Most negotiators counter at this level, and the entire conversation remains at this level. Consider raising the negotiation to the next level, the point at which we can uncover what underlies the stated position. Each of our behaviors and desires usually represents something much deeper in meaning, something that drives the particular behaviors we choose.

A seemingly simple question that has the power to bring the negotiation to a higher level is this: "What is important about that for you?" or, "What will having that do for you?" Notice that these questions ask the other person to look inside himself or herself and provide an indication of what drives the person's stated position.

These questions are not "why" questions and therefore are different from the Chris Matthews inquiry, because the question, "Why?" leads us to hallucinate a response. That is, the mind faces an experience and responds with instinct. The question, "Why?" essentially asks the other person to impute a motive behind his or her behavior, rather than asking to relate a present sense about the position.[4]

If I were to ask Haskell, "*Why* do you want more vacation?" I would likely get a very different response than if I asked, "What is important about having more vacation?" or, "What will that extra week do for you?" The former can trigger defensiveness and asks Haskell to search out a process that is long over. The more present "what" inquiry permits Haskell to offer a reasonable sense about that position. This distinction truly makes a difference.

Assume that Haskell responds, "What is important about the extra vacation is being able to spend more time with my wife, Kay, and our kids." Notice that the response indicates the importance of family and quality time. Isn't it fair to assume that Haskell likely selects many choices based on what will provide him more time with his family? It most certainly is fair.

Uncovering the drives that underlie particular behaviors provides significant insight into that person. People will pursue many behaviors that are driven by the same need; likewise, a particular drive will be responsible for many behaviors. As skilled negotiators, we need to be careful not to assume that the other person is driven by the same things as we are. For example, when Haskell requests additional vacation, we might equate that with laziness or a desire to take advantage of his employer. These are very different factors, and in this case, inaccurate ones, yet it is commonplace for most of us to assume that whatever drives us must be what drives someone else. This simply is not true. Give the other negotiator the respect of being driven by something totally different from that which drives

---

4 Lisnek and Oliver. *Courtroom Power: Communication Strategies for Trial Lawyers.* (PESI Law Publications, 2001).

you; uncover that factor by asking the other person what is important to him or her.

Similarly, we should not assume that two people who share the same driving force also will partake in the same behaviors. One person driven by a sense of responsibility may call clients back within an hour of being called, while another person also driven by responsibility may believe it acceptable to wait a couple days to call a client back. Therefore, when you uncover a driving factor for another person in negotiation, you should not assume that it will lead to any particular behavior. Rather, ask the question that takes the conversation from the underlying level to the behavioral level. The question to ask is, "How do you want that done?" The answer to this question will produce a series of behaviors that are true for that person.

The questions that take a negotiator between the levels of behavior and driving forces are important in a developing negotiation. It should be clear that the skilled negotiator needs to avoid the temptation to impose underlying drives or expected behaviors on the other person. Failure to do so often leads to inaccurate assumptions and faulty positions. Certainly these questions may not produce truthful answers if asked very early in the process; however, once the negotiators settle down to a serious level of conversation, you can expect them to be a bit more up-front in stating some of the underlying needs. The importance of this information should be quite evident in domestic relations disputes, labor strikes, and even in negotiating the sale of a home, as well as establishing salary terms for hiring.

Once we learn what is driving the other person, we are then able to deal with what Fisher and Ury call "the principled position" in their book *Getting to Yes*. Negotiations don't get very far when the participants argue over the components of the positions taken by each negotiator, but can reach resolution when the discussion is focused at the deeper and more meaningful level of motivation, value and goal, and then get there through effective communication. Pay attention to how often negotiators will continue to argue over a specific term or condition. If we could learn that the stated position was grounded with a sense of obligation, or loyalty, we would likely get much further. Sometimes the other negotiator cannot give us what we seek, but he or she can offer us something else that meets the driving need uncovered by finding out what important value really is being represented.

For example, assume that Haskell's boss says he cannot give him an extra week of vacation. Difficulties would then arise, but imagine that the boss adds, "However, knowing your driving need is the desire to spend more time with your family, I would consider discussing flextime and letting you come in a bit later in the day." In other words, Haskell may not get the term he desires, but that term is only reflective of something deeper, and a skilled negotiator can work to meet that need in some way. It is in the combination of identifying underlying or driving needs and in uncovering the terms that meet those needs that the skilled negotiator does his or her finest work.

You Gotta Have Style

Competitive v. Cooperative Negotiators

A ttorney Zach Contursi has been preparing to meet with his boss, Janet Naldo, to discuss his new salary and benefits. He has spent considerable time preparing, evaluating his own needs and wants, deciding how he can best gather information while only strategically releasing information on his own position. In short, Zach has been well in touch with information on salary negotiation. He is now ready to take the next step in his planning, determining what style of negotiation his boss will likely take and what style he will use in response.

Negotiation styles are grounded in our personalities, and we generally adopt strategies that reflect the style. There are two fundamental styles of negotiation: competitive and cooperative. We need to distinguish at the outset the difference between style of negotiation and the strategies that a particular negotiator may employ. That is, a negotiator who is competitive by nature may rely on competitive strategies, but may also call upon seemingly cooperative techniques as well, if that person perceives an advantage to be gained. Similarly, a cooperative negotiator will likely use cooperative strategies, but can resort to competitive techniques if he or she believes that such efforts will move the negotiation in a positive direction. Tactics can be a reflection and component of style, but style is a significantly broader concept than the particular tactics employed. We can use specific tactics to help identify the style of the negotiator.

Much has been written about the importance of style in negotiation. Retired professor Gerald Williams of Brigham Young University Law School focused much of his research in this area on negotiator style. In his critical book, *Legal Negotiation and Settlement*, Williams set out the indicators of negotiator style. There is a clear distinction between the mind-sets of the competitive versus cooperative negotiator. Neither style is better or worse than the other; it is more a matter of effectiveness in the manner in which the styles are enacted.

Competitive negotiators can be identified in the following ways:

- They consistently open a negotiation with an extreme position. Again, because style is neither good nor bad but an issue of effectiveness, the effective negotiator will open with an extreme, but reasonable or at least believable, position. The ineffective competitive negotiator is more likely to open a session with an extreme and unreasonable position. The latter can place the negotiator's credibility into question. How can we know if a position is reasonable or not? The best we can do is monitor our internal reaction to a stated position and learn to monitor the reactions of the person with whom we are negotiating. When a reaction is triggered (verbal or nonverbal) and consciously perceived, as in "You must be crazy!" we have probably reached beyond the level of reason. An inability to support the stated position with underlying (or any) principle is a strong indicator that the stated opening position is not credible.

- They make few concessions, and those that are made tend to be quite stingy. In fact, the competitive negotiator tends to see concessions made by other negotiators as a sign of weakness.

- They argue their position. The competitive negotiator makes emotional and personal attacks, rather than focusing on the parties' interests that underlie those positions. For example, "How can you do this to me, after all the years we've known each other and all the favors I have done for you?" That tactic can go a long way in achieving concessions, if only through guilt.

- They continually challenge the opposition. The competitive negotiator debates every offer presented by the other negotiators.

Cooperative negotiators can be identified by the following factors:

- They make consistent efforts to preserve an effective working relationship between the negotiators.
- They make efforts to identify mutual interests between the negotiators, rather than placing focus on any particular demand.
- They consistently seek out new, creative, and viable options that will meet the interests, needs, and values of all the parties.
- They present options that produce mutual gains for the parties, as opposed to a single-negotiator-focused option.

The interaction is quite interesting when a competitive and cooperative negotiator meet. Here is what Gerry Williams's research indicates:

1. A negotiator with higher aspirations tends to achieve higher rewards through negotiation. Competitive negotiators likely begin at that point; cooperative negotiators should maintain their aspirations, knowing that his or her competitive counterpart will be psychologically fixed on winning.

2. Small concessions produce less failure, or put differently, losers in negotiation make large concessions. Competitive negotiators are geared up for this point, because concession is not in their blood. Effective cooperative negotiators should not and will not fold near the end of a negotiation process, as they hold on to the desire to meet underlying interests.

3. The successful negotiator makes fewer concessions as the deadline nears. Perhaps the best test of the effectiveness

of negotiators is whether they cave in near the end of the process. There may be an actual or imposed deadline, but the effective negotiator will continue to work toward mutually acceptable terms.

4. Cooperative negotiators can distinguish between the styles of negotiator, as competitive negotiators tend to perceive every other negotiator as competitive in style, whether they are or not. This is a fascinating finding, as it suggests that the competitive mind-set sees the efforts of others, including those designed to further the process and seek mutual gain, as competitive. Cooperative negotiators must overcome a pre-existing perception that they are in fact not cooperative, but competitive dressed in cooperative clothing. Cooperative negotiators need to keep a level head and understand that they have an additional two-step task; first, get the competitive negotiator to see the other as cooperative, and second, use cooperative tasks, but make them fit within the competitive mind-set.

It is clearly useful for a negotiator, such as Zach, to consider the style of the negotiator with whom a deal must be struck. If both Zach and Janet are cooperative, they will work together toward a mutually acceptable deal; if one is competitive and the other is cooperative, then they will likely tangle from different perspectives. The cooperative negotiator will attempt to shift the interaction toward underlying interests, and the competitive negotiator will resist any move *away* from his desired position. If both are competitive in style, they will likely just get caught up in a tangle and tussle.

Once the negotiators gather each other's sense of style, they need to make decisions about the particular negotiation arena and employ tactics to take both negotiators toward their goals.

Gonna Sit Right Down and Write Myself a Letter

The Pros and Cons of Negotiating by Phone or Letter

Attorney Eli O'Brien—known for his shrewd negotiations in the entertainment industry—needs to decide whether to set up his next deal through an in-person meeting or whether it is preferable to conduct the session over the telephone. Then again, maybe it is best if he puts his offer and thoughts in writing so that the attorney/agent on the other end of the deal, Ron Lozell, can't confront him over the phone. Although they have negotiated many deals over the past twenty years, they still consider the strategy of how to best put a deal together.

Clearly in-person negotiations bring with them a series of considerations and strategies that have been covered in previous chapters. The handling of negotiations outside an interpersonal interaction raises significant issues for consideration.

There are several advantages to negotiating over the telephone:

1. The interaction is shorter than face-to-face interaction. Over the telephone, negotiators can sidestep the physical positioning and the need to break for lunch (or any other purpose, strategic or not) and simply tend to the business at hand.

2. The caller has the advantage of being prepared. It can be uncomfortable to be on the *receiving* end of a phone call made to initiate a negotiation if you are unprepared. Don't forget famed trial lawyer Johnnie Cochran's advice: the three P's critical to a lawyer...Prepare, Prepare, Prepare! I can't mention or stress this enough. Getting caught unprepared is the worse case scenario for a negotiation (or any other legal task for that matter). Consider asking the caller to reschedule the call or simply indicate that the timing is not satisfactory.

3. It is easier to say no over the telephone or to hang up if the negotiations are not proceeding in a positive direction. Walking out of a face-to-face session can create a disturbance or induce anger. The telephone provides an easier vehicle for buying some time and setting additional discussions for a later time.

4. The telephone reduces the potential for misinterpreting facial expressions. Many people misread visual cues and get confused over the intended message of the negotiator. Over the telephone, it is much easier to concentrate on

words and know that attention needs to be paid to the particular words selected.

5. The telephone permits each party to review confidential information out of the sight of the other party. Many negotiations require you to review key documents you would rather keep out of the sight of the other party. Over the telephone, you have the freedom to look at whatever you need to review without fear of anyone reading over your shoulder.

6. The telephone permits several parties to confer world-wide. The days of deals not being consummated because the parties simply couldn't get together are gone with the increased use of video conference systems (albeit with room for significant technological improvement).

In general, telephone negotiations, used when time is limited and you want the process to move swiftly, can be critical. You just need to figure in some considerations for choosing how *not* to proceed with that telephone negotiation when you are unprepared to do so, for whatever reason. Here are some considerations to mull over:

1. A call can be received when you are not prepared for the negotiation or at an inconvenient time. It is important to take the telephone call when you are ready and not to be pressured at any time. If a deadline is near, then be certain you have reviewed all documents and are ready to proceed.

2. The telephone restricts the amount of input for consideration by removing visual cues that would have been received in person. The converse of reducing misinterpretation through a variety of verbal and nonverbal cues

is the fact that a message minus visual cues is not the whole message. Therefore, a negotiator must attempt to understand the spoken message, the intended message, and the perceived message.

3. You cannot be certain of privacy and security when you are on the telephone. While you control what you can have in front of you in your office during the telephone call, you do not know whether the other negotiator has people listening in to everything you say, potentially unannounced.

4. The use of speakerphones does not yet provide the kind of desirable sound quality (for my taste) of in-person interaction. One day, video technology will be advanced to the stage where it moves at normal speed and with fine picture and sound quality.

Another alternative to in-person and telephone negotiations is to undertake the process in writing. There are advantages to negotiating in writing:

1. Placing positions in writing gives a negotiator the opportunity to reflect on what he or she wishes to commit to writing, as well as the logic and clarity of position. You are provided time to think out and through your position and state it on your chosen terms.

2. Writing reduces the interpersonal dynamics presented by in-person or telephone negotiations. In writing, you cannot be interrupted, cut off, or otherwise distracted from stating your position.

3. Writing helps avoid misunderstanding, but this point is double-edged. In one respect, you can carefully select your language to set out exactly what you wish to say;

conversely, language is ambiguous and all well-intended clarity is sidestepped if the receiver misunderstands the intended message.

Written negotiations are useful when the matter is complex, where confusion is likely, and where a party is concerned that her words will be taken the wrong way. If you select written negotiations, balance these considerations into the decision:

1. While writing provides the drafter with time to reflect on position, it likewise offers the recipient reflection time once the document is received. The spontaneity of interaction is lost, and the receiver has time to respond as he or she wishes.

2. Writing requires more time than personal contact. Conversation permits covering much ground quickly. Interactions in writing mean more time to decide how to approach the other side. By definition, putting offers in writing slows down the process and delays action (although fax machines and email attachments completely negate this concern).

3. Writing arms the recipient for the next contact. Once you read what the other side has to offer, you have time to strategize and plan. Should you respond in writing (in kind) or respond through a telephone call or set up a face-to-face meeting? The writer can be caught off guard if the receiver decides to make a "spontaneous" contact. You can seek to control this consequence by clarifying in the initial document how you wish to be contacted in response; that is, establish the contact rules.

How does one determine whether the best means to conduct a negotiation is in person, over the telephone, or in writing? Rest assured there is no one best method of negotiation; the decision will depend on situation and strategy choices. The bottom line here is that the means for approaching a negotiation must be evaluated, analyzed, and consciously chosen.

Tricks of the Trade

Popular Negotiation Tactics

It's one thing to know what you want, but quite another to calculate the proper moves to achieve it. Attorney Brian Franks has completed an extensive preparation for his salary review, including the stages and styles of negotiation, and now he reviews the tactics available to him for the session. Knowing that it is best to use tactics that are comfortable and natural for him, he reviews the kinds of tactics he has both used and confronted in prior case negotiations. As you consider the list of tactics, remember that not every tactic works for everyone. Evaluate each one with a mind toward ones that fit your style and desired approach.[5] Some of the classic tactics available for consideration include the following:

Puffing on Position

Negotiators often state a position that permits some flexibility for them. The possibility for movement reflects the psychological nature of the process by which each negotiator expects the other to move a bit in position. There is an ethical distinction between suggesting an unwavering position and outright lying. A lawyer has likely crossed the line between permitted puffing and unethical lying when the tools of negotiation cannot reach the truth. Put differently, if a negotiator asks the proper questions, she should be able to get to the truth. A negotiator who holds to a clear lie in the face of direct questions has crossed the line and jeopardizes her credibility.

The effective negotiator should never have to maintain a false position to achieve a desired end; rather, the power of language can be used to create a variety of impressions. Consider those late-night television ads that urge you to "Call before midnight tonight." I am convinced that thousands of people race to their telephones before the witching hour, not realizing that the same ad appears every single evening.

Similarly, in the law, there is a substantive difference between "I cannot see my client accepting that offer" and "My client rejects your offer." If the client authorizes acceptance of the offer along with an attempt to improve the position, then the first comment is acceptable puffing; in it, the lawyer seeks to get a better position but does not actually state a rejection of the offer. The latter comment is more clearly a lie.

---

5   Derived from Lisnek, "Negotiation Power: Winning Skills for Trial Lawyers" (PESI Law Publishing Co., 2004).

The reality is that many people do not hear a substantive difference in the two statements and do not find anything improper about the second statement. The point of this tactic is to highlight that the same end (an improved position or offer for the client) can be accomplished in many different ways. Artful negotiators will use their mastery of language and delivery to create whatever impression they wish to create, yet do so through the skill of puffing, not by crossing the line to lies.

This may be a good time to highlight the ethical requirements on lawyers regarding settlement offers made or offered. Simply put, lawyers must relate every settlement offer they receive in a case to their client unless the client has specifically, and with informed consent, authorized a specific acceptance or rejection range. A client who says, "You have my authority to reject any offer made under $10,000," means that an offer of $5,000 can be rejected without having to relate it to the client. Many lawyers will confirm, however, that they will nevertheless relate any offers received, in the spirit of complete communication with their client. This rule is modified from an older rule that simply required the relating of every settlement offer, regardless; it seems to make little sense to have to relate an offer or demand that has no basis in a realistic world, but nevertheless, that was the requirement.

Expressing Limited Authority

Expressing limited authority is a tactic commonly used by those in the insurance industry or by others who have superiors or supervisors who hold the ultimate (or at least higher) authority. These people state that they have peaked at their authority and cannot move further. True or not? We often don't know. This tactic can be confronted by requiring the person of higher authority to get involved or by being willing to walk from the table until the negotiator representative gets additional authority. But what do you do if you are not able to reach that supervisor? In many settings, such as in the insurance and even the airline industry, when you are at the gate negotiating your way onto a plane with the agent who must call a supervisor, just try getting that supervisor on the phone to talk to you; it won't happen. The answer is not to anger people of limited authority by complaining that they are worthless. Rather, the agents in these cases must become your best friend. They are the gatekeepers to the authority figure, and the best thing you can do is work *with* them. Ask questions such as this: "What would the supervisor need to change her position on this point? What is important to her? Has she exceeded this limit in the past?" You may be surprised to find that the gatekeeper who likes you is also willing to assist you in crafting a position to persuade the person with authority.

Anger

Less a tactic than a disruption when real, feigned anger can be effective to shake someone from a position. When the anger is real, the negotiator may be less in control of what he is saying; but when controlled or strategic, the use of anger can often produce a shift. This tactic can be confronted by matching the behavior, thereby letting the first negotiator know that he must back off that tactic, because it does little more than escalate the disagreement.

One-Up, One-Down

Under the one-up, one-down tactic, whatever point you put out during the negotiation discussion, the other negotiator finds it necessary to "one-up," or better your point. This can be frustrating when you are attempting to make a point, only to have the other person respond simply by bettering your story or point. To stop the response, you might try challenging the one-up by interrogating that person on the point and then seeking to return the focus onto your position. It is also useful to recognize that people who consistently respond to a story with a one-up are not digesting the information being related to them; rather, they are remaining internally focused on their own ego. Proceed with that type of person accordingly. You may need to suspend the negotiations awhile until they are a bit more willing to listen.

Take It or Leave It

"My best offer first" is a tactic developed years ago in labor law. It is effectively used only by those who mean it, those who will follow through and have the authority to do what they say they will do. A famous example is President Reagan's threat to fire all air traffic controllers back in the 1980s when the union was on strike for an extended period of time. Reagan threatened to fire all controllers if they did not accept his best-offer position. With few people believing the president would actually take such a drastic step, the offer was rejected by the union. The result made history when the president followed through and fired the air traffic controllers, permanently and never to be re-hired. Another infamous example was the year of the baseball strike in the 1990s when the baseball negotiations were caught in a no-shift position. Many people thought either the team owners or the players would give in—after all, we couldn't possibly cancel a World Series. It had never happened in the history of baseball! This stubborn position, underlain with actual authority by the negotiators, did what two world wars and even a major earthquake could not do, cancel the World Series.

If you do not have the authority to follow through on a take it or leave it position, you quickly lose credibility, and few people are likely to fear or take seriously other similar uses of the tactic. To confront the tactic, be prepared to walk from the table and face the consequences, ignore the tactic and try to refocus the discussion, or attempt to reframe the position for the user of the tactic to illustrate why that tactic would not accomplish what that person desires. This is not a tactic to be used or taken lightly, because in the long run the user's credibility as a negotiator is truly put on the line, and once lost, reputation cannot usually be recouped.

Silence

Silence is a powerful tool because so few people can actually sit silently in the face of another person's silence, yet it is exactly what you must do when someone uses silence as a tactic. In most cases, the existence of silence will trigger the other person to start talking, to possibly start conceding, or to otherwise make the next move. Next time, just sit there, silently, until the user of the tactic feels that same pressure to speak. The tactic will soon get set aside once everyone realizes that no one is talking at all, and soon someone will begin to fill the silence, as most human beings want to do.

The Snow-Job

The snow-job tactic refers to the use of alleged but, in fact, false expertise on a particular topic. Many of us confront people who talk and talk but likely do not have the substantive knowledge behind them. You are best advised to confront the tactic by asking questions, interrogating, exploring the information, and forcing the self-styled expert's hand on the issue.

Mutt and Jeff

The Mutt-and-Jeff technique is used in a team negotiation. One negotiator seeks additional concessions from the other party by pointing to some *other* person of authority who is not even present in the negotiations, yet is referred to as a key decision maker. In effect, the negotiator says, "I can accept what you are saying, but my partner Mutt, back at the office, will never go for that. Can you improve your position a bit for Mutt, and by the way, I personally really appreciate your openness and willingness to resolve this matter." The best way to confront the tactic is to seek out Mutt, and invite him or her to participate in the process.

It is difficult to negotiate with someone you do not see. Isn't that one benefit of keeping negotiations between the lawyers and not letting clients go back and forth with each other, thereby working *around* the lawyers? It is also why mediators and judges will often ask clients to be personally present at settlement conferences, because it is more likely that an agreement can be reached when everyone with authority is made a part of the process.

Splitting the Difference

Splitting the difference is one of my favorite tactics *not* to use! Many negotiators will attempt to create guilt whenever the other negotiator does not agree to split the difference. The classic situation goes like this: "We have offered $1,000, and you need $1,500; let's meet in the middle and agree to $1,250, okay?" How do you say no to that offer? You would appear to be unfair, and even a person of bad character, if you said no, wouldn't you? Well, keep in mind that this offer to split the difference is nothing more than a negotiation tactic. You are not required to meet anyone halfway, even if it does make most people feel good. With supporting principle and a strong position, a negotiator can refuse to compromise to the halfway point. An approach quite comfortable for the competitive negotiator, it may appear less appealing for the negotiator who relies on the give-and-take. You may have to respond, "I understand why you want to meet halfway, as we both give a little and lose some as well, but I cannot do that, and let me explain why that is the case. We have more money in this process than $1,250 so we can't go that low; the number just doesn't work for us." What is wrong with that response to someone who wishes to force a settlement by meeting in the middle? Nothing.

Once an agreement is reached, it will most always be reduced to writing, or in most cases *should* be reduced and memorialized in writing. It is seemingly a simple task to place or commit already agreed-upon terms on paper, yet this task often becomes a challenge and hotbed for dispute even after the terms have been reached.

It Ain't Over 'til the Fat Lady Sings

Drafting the Final Negotiation Agreement

Attorneys Tim Jones of Mertz, Maude, and Matthews, and Kristofer Fridgen of Parker, Crosbie, and Charles have finally come to terms after several months of ongoing negotiations. The business deal will finally close, and each party wants to be certain that the agreement is drafted with care and caution. This article in the negotiation series discusses the importance of careful drafting of a negotiated agreement.

In general, a viable agreement will lead the parties to be satisfied with the methods and processes employed by the negotiators and also the content of the agreement. Because negotiation is a psychological process, the parties need to be comfortable with the tangible and intangible results of the process and resulting deal.

When drafting the agreement, it is essential that you do the following:

- Confirm the terms. It is amazing how much can change between the conclusion of the negotiation discussions and the written agreement. Whether intentionally or not, written agreements can be drafted with errors and changes that materially shift the meaning of the document. Before drafting the agreement, the parties should review each and every term. This action will at least ensure that the fundamental terms are likely to appear in the agreement, although the potential for modification remains.

- Do not delegate the task to another person. It always seems easier to have someone else take care of the task of drafting. In my days as a defense lawyer, it was not uncommon for the plaintiff's counsel to ask me to draft the agreement, because I was paid by the hour. This tactic, essentially, is a strategic mistake. The drafter has significant power and influence in the manner in which the terms appear and potentially get enforced. It has happened on more than one occasion in my career that an agreement drafted by someone else ended up including terms that materially modified the agreement. If you don't catch the changes, you can expect to be stuck with the results.

- Review the agreement carefully for accuracy. This means reading beyond the wording of the major terms. Sometimes one additional term or twist of phrase can change expectations, responsibilities, and enforcement.

- Be certain that the agreement terms are specific. Dates, times, and other specific expectations should be kept as unambiguous as possible. Phrases such as "at a reasonable time" work in some instances, but not all. Remember, there are people who hire lawyers just for the purpose of finding a loophole or other means of getting out of the legal responsibilities of a previously reached agreement.

- Be certain the terms are flexible. Clearly, the reason the U.S. Constitution has remained in force and effect for hundreds of years is because of its flexibility and openness to interpretation. Keep an eye toward the future as you draft the agreement. What may work today may not be effective tomorrow. Without a crystal ball, how can we work to ensure flexibility for the future? Initially, you can expect that the most difficult planning for the future will be in the areas such as price, time, and dates. No one knows what the future holds, so it is difficult to predict economic factors. (I don't even trust the Fed to do that accurately.) Consider the case of that great actress Dianne Carroll, who once purchased an apartment in New York City with the condition that she agree to sell that apartment back to a particular party at the price she paid for the unit (about $20,000 at the time). The unit's value increased to several hundred thousand dollars, and she found herself in a lawsuit requesting the court to find the contract unconscionable. If only she had known decades earlier what was going to happen to the price of real estate in New York! A more viable approach at the time might have been to tie the promised purchase price to a percentage of current market value at the time of sale. This is the kind of foresight we need to bring when translating verbal terms to enforceable writing.

- Strive for simplicity. Sometimes legalese is necessary to remove ambiguity; other times it serves to create a document so incomprehensible that no one can make heads or tails out of its intention or function. Wherever possible, use simple, clear terms so that the parties (and others) who need to read, execute, and abide by the agreement can do so.

- Be certain to make the agreement operational. It is most unfortunate to draft an agreement that covers all of the material terms except how the agreement will be activated. Be certain that a starting time or event is specified to ensure that the parties actually do what they are required by the contract to do. Demanding that a condition be completed "as soon as practicable" may suggest urgency, but it also can be read to permit procrastination. I recall a case where the parties fought for more than a year to reach an agreement. The relationships remained sour, but one day one of them seemingly gave in, and an agreement was drafted. It was months later when the other party noted that the terms of the agreement were not being complied with by the first party and inquired as to what the problem might be. "Oh, when does that agreement say we will do that item?" Upon review, the other side noted no operational term. "Huh, I guess we didn't specify a date." The other person responded, "Exactly! When hell freezes over, we'll do this deal!" They never had come to terms but pushed the situation to this edge, and in the end, no agreement was actually reached, then or ever, by the way.

- Include provisions and contingencies for compliance. A party may have a good reason for *not* completing a required term. The agreement should address such a contingency and specify how compliance with the terms can otherwise be achieved.

- Include provisions for change. Coupled with the suggestion to think about necessary flexibility in terms, it is important for the parties to look ahead and recognize that things change; times change and conditions change. When this happens, the agreement should provide contingencies that keep it viable and enforceable.

- Include provisions for handling potential disputes. Inclusion of an alternative dispute resolution mechanism in the case of disagreement or challenge is essential. My personal opinion and suggestion is for that provision to be one that requires mediation, rather than arbitration or some other proceeding. Mediation is the only form of ADR that permits the parties, with the assistance and guidance of a trained mediator, to reach their own terms for agreement. This process allows the parties to own the agreement. The probabilities for success following the mediation increase significantly, because it is a process not imposed on the parties, but rather one that involves them.

- Think of and approach the memorializing of every negotiation as the most important part of the process. The absence of a well-drafted agreement can mean that a great deal of hard negotiating and coming to terms may be for naught. The final drafting is not the time to check out of the process. The final written agreement is what all parties must live by, and in the event of a problem, for any person who seeks to resolve the dispute (be it an ADR professional, judge, or jury), it will be the starting and ending point of interpretation. Take good care in drafting, and the probabilities for success are as high as they can be. The net result is a satisfied client and a prosperous lawyer.

> *Whether the focus of your negotiation is your own salary, your client's well-being, or your own purchases, whether in litigation or transactional work, it is clear that negotiation requires skill and finesse. Keep your attention on the process and the people, not on their positions. In the words of Mark Twain, if you do what is right, you will gratify some and astonish the rest.*

Mediate before You Litigate

The Importance of Alternative Dispute Resolution

Because more than 90% of civil cases settle before trial, it is clear that lawyers recognize litigation to verdict as less than the best road to resolution. In days when lawyers are urged to be more civil with each other and the system, we witness an increasing use of mediation.

The process uses the skills of a neutral third party who intervenes in a dispute to assist the parties in finding their own resolution. Mediators do not make findings of fact or law, as a judge or an arbitrator would do; rather they facilitate an open discussion between the parties about their own needs and interests. The process relies on active participation from the parties and their lawyers.

While alternative dispute resolution tools are well-tried alternatives to arguing in court, attorneys still do not use the process of mediation readily. Perhaps it is because lawyer training emphasizes adversarial tactics over mutual resolution, but the more likely explanation lies in attorney inexperience and unfamiliarity with the process. In addition, mediation's relative youth, at least compared to other forms of alternative dispute resolution, means that few people understand its benefits or know how the process works.

The benefits of mediation are many and include the following:

- It is less time consuming than litigation. Court backlogs suggest that even people who can afford the high cost of litigation wait years for their day in court. A mediation session can be arranged quickly and produce resolution in hours, most often in less than a day.

- It is much less expensive than litigation.

- It includes exploring alternatives. Unlike a "fixed pie" distribution that litigation produces, mediation focuses on flexible solutions; it "expands the pie of opportunity."

- It addresses the needs of all the parties. By definition, a consensual agreement reached through mediation will reflect the parties' needs, because all parties will have played a role in the crafting of that agreement. The same cannot be said for verdicts at trial.

- It improves communication among all the parties. Litigation fosters an adversarial environment that is not conducive to effective communication. A trained professional mediator interrupts this escalation and replaces it with assistance to communicate.

- It increases the probability of compliance. Disagreement as to the term of an imposed settlement or judgment reduces the probability of compliance. Because a mediated solution is an agreed-upon product emerging from the parties themselves, it is more likely to be followed.

In general, mediation will move through five stages. During the first stage, the mediator *establishes the guidelines and tone* for the session. These rules promote fairness and equality among the parties and highlight the cooperative nature of the session. The rules might be as simple as not interrupting while others are speaking and as structural as when and how breaks are scheduled and where the parties should sit.

The next stage is *fact finding*. The parties each relate their version of the underlying facts to the mediator who listens, knowing that the truth likely lies somewhere in between the competing accounts. The mediator seeks to identify areas of disagreement and works to develop trust among the parties and the mediator. Caucus meetings for information gathering and trust building are a tool that is unique to mediation. In a caucus, the mediator meets privately with each party to explore and encourage acceptance of the other party's perspective. In addition, candid and realistic perspectives are shared in this private confidential setting, which is provided equally to all parties.

The third stage is the development of *settlement options*. Parties discuss their positions and suggest alternatives in an effort to have all of their demands met. They brainstorm for possible solutions that satisfy both stated and unstated needs.

The mediator uses information gathered in caucus, while maintaining confidentiality, as the process proceeds.

Deciding on the *best option* is the fourth stage of the process. The parties focus on the alternatives that best satisfy each other's interest at the least cost to all the parties. Having built a foundation of trust and good faith, here the parties negotiate, compromise, and trade off concessions to arrive at a tentative agreement. The mediator encourages the parties and their lawyers to formulate an agreement and ensures that everyone is heard.

Lastly, the mediator assists parties and their lawyers to *formalize the agreement*, memorializing in writing the list of options to which both parties agreed. Most often, the lawyers write the agreement in language that everyone understands, avoiding legalese and language barriers inevitably found in litigated resolutions. It is not an easy task for a lawyer to draft something that does not look and sound lawyerly, but how nice it is for the laypeople who need to live by the agreement!

If you take part in a mediation as a party or lawyer representing a party, be certain that the mediator has undergone proper training and perhaps holds a certification as a mediator. It is unfortunate but true that some retired judges and lawyers rely a bit too much on arm twisting the parties to reach an agreement. It is not easy for someone who is trained in and lives in a world of advocacy to put that aside and implement a more conciliatory style. I draw a clear distinction between facilitation and browbeating, not that every mediator does not have the best intentions. They do, but the effective mediator guides the parties through the process, assisting everyone to see more options. The agreement, however, must belong to the parties.

Although mediation is non-adversarial by definition, attorneys play an important role as counsel. First, they advise their client as to the viability of litigation. Once most clients are made aware of the costs and delays of a litigated solution, they are more dedicated to valuable participation in the mediation. In addition, lawyers ensure that any terms agreed to through mediation are equitable to their client and also that they are drafted in a way that conforms to the intent and reasonable expectations of the client.

It is true that not every dispute is appropriate for mediation, although most can be resolved through the process. There are times when litigation is needed to resolve major policy questions or to establish precedent. In other words, the conflict in some cases reaches well beyond the parties and affects all of society. This would be every case that reaches the U.S. Supreme Court, for example. Of course, these cases are few in number. That being said, when there is flexibility in the solution, and where the participants take the process seriously, then mediation is most likely going to be successful.

If you have not yet tried mediation, you can count on a pleasant surprise. If you have participated in mediation, then help spread the word, because its well-deserved day is already here.

Arbitrate like You Litigate

Suggestions for an Effective Arbitration

I made it clear in the previous article that mediation is a great tool for resolving disputes without having to resort to the courtroom for a trial. Mediation does not always work, for reasons that may include clients who are not willing to work with each other toward a resolution. Before the lawyer puts the time, money, and stress into a lengthy protracted jury trial, though, may I suggest that arbitration be considered as another means to reach a speedy resolution. This process permits lawyers to advocate on behalf of their clients, gives clients their "day in court," so to speak, and produces a result or decision in a timely fashion. I have worked for many years as an arbitrator in personal injury and a few securities cases and take this opportunity to offer some suggestions on how lawyers and their clients might fare better in the process.

I have to be honest; I sit as an arbitrator, and more often than not, I am astonished at the poor performances I see by lawyers who are supposedly representing a client in a zealous manner, so while I point to the value and benefits of arbitration, it is critical that the players put as much preparation and effort into this procedure as they would into a trial. I see lawyers who are unprepared, who ask cross-examination questions that do no more than confirm what was stated on direct, and who in the name (perhaps) of economy, proceed with arguments absent substantive or responsive testimony in support of their position. Sound incredible? I think so too, every time I experience it, and I experience it far more often than I should.

As an arbitrator, my job is to hear the arguments and the evidence and then render a decision much as would a judge or jury in a trial setting. I also expect the lawyers who appear before me to do a fine job on behalf of their clients, though. What I find more often than not is that a lawyer who represents a respondent corporate entity, such as an insurance carrier in an uninsured motorist case, attends the hearing with file in hand, but absent a sword or shield. The claimants in such cases are prepared to put on their case. The party is always present and provides testimony. Rarely, if ever, does the respondent insurance carrier offer any contrary evidence, either on the issue of liability or on damages. It relies, instead, on the art of cross-examination, and while it may be okay with the insurance carrier when the amount at risk is only $20,000 or maybe

$40,000 for two claimants, on some level the company must have decided that the cost to defend the case with expert testimony and such isn't justified by the aggregate amount at risk. From my perspective, though, they also decided not to settle the case for a sum of money that may have been less than the cost to defend it and so proceed to the arbitration, but I still suggest that you be prepared to defend your case with evidence I can consider, and not just conjecture or suggestion.

What do I typically see at such proceedings? I see a lawyer who cross-examines the claimant as though that lawyer has no real plan of attack. "So are you really that hurt?" "You say you didn't see the car coming from behind?" They do little more on cross than repeat what was testified to on direct examination, because I believe they don't have any real direction to take the testimony. I suggest they simply waive the cross and let the testimony stand where it may. In one recent case, a claimant asked if she could offer information that no one had asked her. When I explained she could answer only the questions posed by the lawyers, her lawyer followed by asking her what it was that she wanted to say. She talked about a sporting competition she had to forgo as a result of her injury, but no one had asked her about it. Her lawyer let the testimony simply stand without much development, but then counsel for the respondent insurer decided to cross on the point. That defense lawyer asked her about the amount of registration fees paid and learned that they were not refunded, among other points. I found it interesting that it was the defense lawyer who was strengthening the claimant's case, even where her own lawyer failed to do so. After a series of questions, this point finally seemed to occur to the respondent. He paused, looked at me, and said, "I think I am just helping their case. I'll stop here." Good idea, dude.

The lawyers who appear before me seem to rely on the fact that I too am a lawyer, and that I know a credible (or incredible) story when I hear one. Mostly, the defense arguments encourage me to use my experience and common sense to see that the claimant is lying, exaggerating, and puffing, but they offer me no admissible evidence to the contrary. Sometimes a good claimant's lawyer will state, "Mr. Arbitrator, you don't get to ignore the evidence and just assume what their expert testimony *would* have been had they presented any. You have to make your decision based on the evidence presented into the record and not on the basis of innuendo, assumption, or conjecture." How true. I think that respondent lawyers believe that I will just ignore the evidence and not require the respondent to actually do their job. That's not how I reach my decisions. Sometimes I want to speak up and say, "Hey, defense lawyer, don't you get that you need to challenge this point?" or "Where is your evidence to contradict the damages demand? You can't just *say* it's inflated; you gotta show me!" I don't say such things, though, because in my view, that's not my job or responsibility.

Arbitration, when handled properly, is an efficient and effective tool to save parties a great deal of time, heartache, and stress as they wait for and then have to live through trial. Often handled in an afternoon, simple cases can be presented and argued and a decision rendered that will be reasonable and appropriate. The backlog of cases that so many jurisdictions face each year needs to be resolved. Arbitration presents a wonderful means to plow through cases using people who are trained and qualified to hear such matters, and it avoids the intimidation of the courtroom setting, including the possible arrogance of a judge. All in all, arbitration is more likely than not going to produce an equitable result in a much shorter period of time than waiting for one's day in court.

Like many of my colleague lawyers, I love the courtroom and all its challenges. I recognize that many lawyers crave the opportunity to give that Clarence Darrow-like closing argument, but the realities of the system are such that we must work together to clear up the ever-growing backlog of cases. Address those cases in the system that can be resolved without muddling their way through the complexities of the entire chronology of a lawsuit; experience much of the same excitement offered by a trial through the processes offered by arbitration. In more cases than not, you'll be glad you did.

PART III.

DISCOVERING REALITY

A LOOK AT DEPOSITIONS

Testimony
Stipulations

All too often a case that comes in the door looks too good. Our client seemingly is without fault, and it appears to be a slam-dunk. The day of reckoning arrives, and we realize that there are many other sides to the story our client failed to relate. It's not that clients mean to misguide their lawyer; they just show up with unavoidable biases and tainted memories. We need to test the realities presented to us before we march through discovery on our way to trial. A sensitivity to bias plays a key role throughout the entire litigation process, as this next series of articles illustrates.

Memories Can Improve with Age

Gathering Accurate Recollections

Lawyer Rick Duffy is frustrated at how much his client's story has changed from the time she first came into his office. His client, Karen Jillians, is in a contract battle with Floppy Inc. over the delivery of certain goods. Emotional at first, Karen told Rick several facts that later proved to be misstated and overstated. Rick was thrown because it made sense to him that memories are sharper the closer they are to the events; the more time went on, the more distorted memories become.

This experience raises an interesting question: When is our memory the most sharp, clear, and, most importantly, accurate?

At first glance, it would appear that a person's memory is best nearest to the event in question. After all, this is the closest moment in time to the event there is; anything later would necessarily suffer from the changes and reinterpretations that occur in our minds. The natural process called slippage means that once an event is over, we begin to delete certain details from our minds and add others to our memory. This process helps us fit an event into our existing set of values and attitudes.

For example, if we are involved in a car accident, most of us immediately find a way to blame the other person or anything else we can find that helps us displace the blame. Over time, our memory includes our looking both ways before entering the intersection, seeing everything that a safe driver would see, and taking every precaution expected of a good driver. Did all this really happen? Probably not, but our minds will integrate these new facts and delete contrary ones with such power that our reality changes. It would therefore appear that memories are better closest to the event, before slippage sets in to taint the experience. This is likely why insurance investigators work speedily to get statements from insureds as close to the time of an accident as possible, so that they can pin down memories.

Further reconsideration, however, indicates that the memories related close to the time of the event are the furthest away from the realities that will be proven at the time of trial.

The details that get gathered close to the event are often confused and internally contradictory, even in the mind of the person relating the information. We think we looked both ways, but the other car came out of nowhere, or we thought the contract language was clear, but we never considered the consequence that eventually occurred. It is easy enough to see how our memories are incorrect at the time of the event, but what supports the notion that our memories actually improve over time?

The answer rests not in the memory of the client but in the totality of information gathered from other statements, documents, and evidence. Once there is sufficient time to review all the evidence gathered, it becomes possible for the lawyer to sit down with the client and say, essentially, "Your memory cannot be correct. We have sufficient contrary information that proves it couldn't have happened that way," or, "Six other witnesses saw the car approaching the intersection, so it didn't come out of nowhere. We need to discuss where else you may have been looking besides to the right and left as you stated previously."

Given objective proof, most people are willing to accept that their memories are in fact tainted and that they may have to back off, at least to the point of saying "I don't remember" at the time of deposition or trial.

Lawyers should caution their clients, whenever possible, against giving statements too early in a case and before a review of all existing tangible evidence and witness accounts. Too much time is spent rehabilitating clients from statements made early on that prove to be untrue by the time of deposition and then trial. The less said early on, the better.

What steps can be taken to gather information properly from a client?

1. Get an uninterrupted account from the client. Find out whether the client has given any previous statement, and be certain to review that statement with the client. Learn the basis and support for each comment made in that statement.

2. Ask the client what tangible evidence or witnesses exist that could be relevant; that is, could confirm or back up the statements given by that client.

3. Review all evidence gathered and evaluate the validity of the client's statement. Address each inconsistency directly with the client. Do not move on to a new point unless the client can disprove or otherwise explain the contrary evidence or gain comfort with the new understanding of adjusted events and memory.

The strange part of the trap that gets set in early statements that are challenged later on is that many people were only trying to be honest and helpful at the time of the original comments. Few people look ahead to the possibility of impeachment and are often surprised that much of what they recall is not accurate. If you believe in the philosophy that no good deed goes unpunished, then you understand the need to bail out many a client from the memories he or she relates early on in the case.

When confronted with contradictory evidence, clients should not be afraid to admit that their memories were less than perfectly accurate or exact. In fact, given all that I have discussed above, every client should anticipate challenges to previously related memories. At the time of deposition, the client should state with confidence and in all good faith, "At the time of my original statement, I remembered the light being green. Since that time, I have come to learn that the lights were *flashing* green." The lawyer's task is twofold: to ensure that acknowledging contrary facts doesn't throw the client, and second, to review the events with the client so that they can be related in a consistent, coherent, and complete manner.

In a difficult case, the lawyer should keep the main point of this column in mind for opening statement or closing argument. Because the "improvement" of memory over time is contrary to expectation, it makes sense to point this fact out directly to the jury:

How is it, ladies and gentlemen, that my client's story has shifted over time? Does the truth really change over time? In the effort to be as candid and honest as possible, my client gave a statement immediately after the event, and now my opponent wishes to paint a shift in that account as being an intentional lie. The reality, ladies and gentlemen, is that my client always has made and continues to make every effort to relate these events as best she can remember them.

By explaining the process of how memory works, the jury can understand the message and continue to find the client credible, even in the face of a challenge.

Do not fear the passage of time as you work up a case. Put faith in your ability to confirm details, and work with clients to present the most consistent account possible at the subsequent times of deposition or trial.

Writing the Story
for Trial

Taking Effective Depositions

"Cover that deposition for me, will ya?" or "Just find out what she knows; that's all." These all-too-commonly made statements are the instructions given to many less-experienced lawyers as they are sent off to take a deposition, yet if the process were so easy, why do so many seasoned trial lawyers find themselves frustrated at the time of trial when the depositions taken in the case don't support the case theme or story ultimately desired to be related to a jury at trial? The answer rests in the all-too-forgotten connection between depositions and the trial story.

The trial story does not begin at the moment trial preparation begins. Law school teaches us well enough that we should draft our closing argument first, before any other trial planning, but the closing argument is compromised if the pretrial discovery cannot support it. In short, we are best advised to draft the closing argument shortly after the completion of the initial attorney-client interview and to begin crafting its support through the course of discovery and especially through depositions.

Depositions are more than information-gathering devices that help us explore and probe what a deponent says. They must reach further into both case strategy and design. Depositions offer the opportunity to evaluate the witness's appearance for determining how that person will testify at trial. In addition, depositions provide an opportunity for lawyers to evaluate the style and approach of the other lawyers as well. All this information can be integrated into case strategy and the determination of the techniques that may work in court and those that won't.

Most important, however, is the use of the deposition to test and evaluate the story to be told at trial. Consider where your case needs to end up when you first take it into the office, and you are likely to find that your stories have new strength and appeal by the time trial actually takes place. Ultimately a jury is going to evaluate how complete, coherent, and consistent each side's story is through testimony, evidence, and argument.

Sliding a story through in the face of deposition testimony that contradicts the trial story places two burdens on the lawyer. First, the lawyer must find a technique to explain away the contradictory deposition testimony, and second, the lawyer must convince the jury that the testimony presented at trial is more credible than the information gathered at the prior deposition. These tasks would seem unnecessary if the lawyers gave more thought to what was to be accomplished at the deposition.

Use the deposition to test the story you begin developing from the first time you interview the plaintiff or receive the file for defense. We have the right to use leading questions in adversarial depositions, but we use this form of questioning all too little. Leading questions are an essential tool to limiting a deponent's testimony, controlling its development, and exposing its weaknesses. Of course, to be effective in the use of leading questions, you need to have a sense of the case story you are seeking to develop.

True, through strategic and effective questioning, the other side will come to learn the nature of the story you plan to tell at trial. Some lawyers may criticize as harmful the consequence of letting the other side know what their own trial story is going to be, but I ask, where's the harm? After all, no one will ever really know what happened back at the time of the events anyway. All we can ever hope to do is create a credible and powerful *current* accounting of past events for the decision maker or finder of fact.

If our case has a weakness, wouldn't we much rather have the other side point it out to us *now*? In fact, I invite my opponent to illustrate through his or her own questioning or challenges to my examination where the weaknesses in my case lie, where the inconsistencies emerge, and where I need to fill a gap. Better that we learn of these problems early on in the case rather than to wait until the trial date, or worse yet wait until the evidence at trial illustrates that our case is riddled with problems.

Does it not make more sense to be building a case story from the very first gathering of discovery materials? Shouldn't we have a sense of our story from the first telling of the account by our client during an interview? True enough, we'll need to modify the account, perhaps constantly, as new pieces of information come to us. Knowing that every account of an event is related through the tainted and biased memories of our clients, consider the insight we gain into the nature of how our clients tend to bias their reporting of information by having them draft out their story at the onset of a case and then seeing how additional information comes in. For the lawyer, it means drafting out the closing argument at the beginning of the case and then seeing, as time goes on, whether the evidence supports the arguments made at that time.

For example, suppose your client comes to see you about a breach-of-contract case. Assume that she tends to focus her comments on the bad attitudes of the other parties and their unwillingness to work out the conflict. You draft a closing argument that reflects that point, but come to learn through discovery that the opposite is true. It appears to be your own client, and not the other parties, who was seemingly unreasonable in attempting to achieve a resolution. This way, you learn that your client tends to bias her reporting of other people's demeanor and communication style. This may be a concern regarding other relationships that are relevant to the case.

If you don't use this approach, then future depositions taken by lawyers who "just seek to find out what you know" may miss the demeanor and attitude components of the interaction. By drafting a closing argument in story form at the onset of the case, every lawyer who takes part in working up the file can gain the same insights and knowledge about the case as it builds through each deposition. The benefits gained by drafting a story at the outset of a case are tremendous and can produce a significantly higher level of competence in trial preparation.

To summarize this storytelling approach, you should proceed in the following manner:

1. Interview the client if you are a plaintiff's lawyer or review the case file for the defense.

2. Draft the case story that could be given as a closing argument at that time. This task includes a consideration of what other evidence and testimony will be needed to support and strengthen the case story as it exists at that time.

3. With each set of interrogatory responses, each production request, and each deposition, consider its effects and impact on the case story. Modify the story as necessary to keep it complete, consistent, and coherent for a jury. If clearly contradictory information to the story emerges, then work to clear it up through future discovery, and if you cannot, then you will need to change that part of the case story that cannot be supported so that it re-establishes the necessary consistent account.

By the time the trial comes along, your case story will have undergone significant modification and analysis. You also will be quite ready to begin your trial presentation already knowing that your trial account is supported by the evidence.

If They're "Usual," Why Don't I Know What They Are?

The Usual Stipulations of Depositions

New attorney Chip Douglas has the uncomfortable moment one has after the introductory amenities of a deposition. The court reporter asks whether the parties agree to the usual stipulations. "What stipulations?" asks Chip. Although not certain what to do, he agrees, because the label "usual" makes them sound safe enough. At least Chip is in good company. The odds are that no one else at the deposition has a clue to what these stipulations are either!

It makes sense to have reservations regarding deposition stipulations. They vary among locales and raise a range of issues among different lawyers. Whatever is agreed to by the lawyers should be spelled out by the court reporter in the record. What exactly are the potential stipulations to which we agree? They can include any of the following:[6]

1. Agreeing that the deposition will be taken in accordance with the Federal Rules of Civil Procedure. This is a relatively harmless stipulation, because these rules govern the interaction whether or not the parties agree to them.

2. Agreeing to reserve all substantive or evidentiary objections until trial. Certainly, Rule 32(b) of the Federal Rules of Civil Procedure indicates such, even in the absence of this stipulation; however, objections as to the form of a question need to be made concisely and in a non-argumentative manner at the time of the deposition (Rule 30 (d)).

3. Agreeing to waive the oath. This agreement would contradict Rule 30(c), which requires the officer before whom the deposition is to be taken to administer an oath or affirmation. The absence of an oath would undermine the impeachment power of the deposition. Imagine the embarrassment of attempting to impeach a witness at trial who responds to the question, "And you were under oath to tell the truth, weren't you?" with, "No, I was not sworn in at the deposition."

4. Agreeing to waive the reading and signing of the transcript pursuant to Rule 30(e). This stipulation is best avoided. Many lawyers routinely waive the reading and signing of the transcript, believing that only technical

6 *Depositions: Procedure, Strategy and Technique.* 3rd ed. Paul Lisnek and Michael Kaufman. (Thomson West Publishing Co., 2006).

transcription errors may be corrected. Quite to the contrary, Rule 30(c) permits thirty days from the time of notice that the transcript or recording is available to review and make changes in form or substance. As a presenting lawyer, it is best to reserve the opportunity to review the interaction later.

Consider how often another lawyer covers a deposition for us. A review of the transcript often indicates a misstatement or some other change the responsible lawyer sees as necessary and appropriate in the transcript. Waiving the right waives the chance to make the change. True, changes made to the transcript permit the deposing lawyer to re-depose on those changes, but this exposure may be far less of a concern than the preservation of incorrect and dangerous testimony. Moreover, there is great power in the impeachment of a deponent with a transcript that has been reviewed for its accuracy.

Consider the trial interaction when lawyer Douglas asks, "And you had the opportunity to review the transcript and make any changes you wished; isn't that correct?" "Yes, I did," responds the deponent. "But you made no changes to the accuracy of the transcript as I read it to you here," Douglas says.

This power can be enhanced by recognizing the power in Federal Rule 30(e) for the deponent or any party to exercise the right to have the deponent read and sign the transcript. Often thought to belong only to the deponent, the right can be exercised by any party, thus enhancing the moment of impeachment. "And you had the right to read and change the transcript? In fact, I gave you that right by requesting that you ensure your testimony was accurate, yet you still made no changes."

Is there risk in having the deponent read a transcript where a wonderful admission is gained? Sure. The real risk is that the deponent will *actually read* the transcript! The reality is that few deponents will read the transcript carefully, if at all, and the likelihood is low that any changes will be made. Nevertheless, the strategic decision must balance the achieved admission with its powerful impeachment and the risk of change through review.

5. Agreeing that withdrawn questions will be omitted from the final transcript. A worthwhile stipulation; the record is kept clean and transcription costs are reduced. On the other hand, lawyers often leak thoughts of strategy and direction through a question that is then stricken. There may be value in studying potential question or trial strategies that may appear in the deposing lawyer's questions.

6. Agreeing that any attorney's objection shall suffice as though every attorney had made the objection. A valuable stipulation, this reduces the interruptions to the interaction and ensures that every lawyer has standing or can argue the objection before the judge. Without the stipulation, the lawyer defending the objection can attempt to keep all but the objecting lawyer from participating, claiming the others have no standing with regard to that objection. The stipulation resolves this issue.

7. Agreeing that an instruction from lawyer to deponent not to answer a question equals the client deponent's not answering the question. This stipulation saves the time of walking through the many steps to certify a question. The

usual and complete process would be to ask the question, hear an objection, repeat the question to have the deponent confirm that he or she will not answer the question on the advice of counsel, and then certify the question. The stipulation permits the question to be certified upon the lawyer's first instruction that the client will not be answering the question. Clearly, this stipulation applies when the deponent is represented by counsel, but arguably not when an independent deponent testifies without counsel present.

I do not like to agree to this stipulation, based on an experience I had when deposing a lawyer in a disciplinary proceeding. The lawyer had been accused of forging, among other things, his wife's signature on a contract. In previous settings, the lawyer had taken the fifth and refused to answer any questions. When I posed the question in the disciplinary hearing, the respondent's lawyer spoke his usual instruction, "I am instructing you not to answer that question," but rather than stopping there, I repeated the question, expecting the respondent to follow the advice of counsel. The reality is that whether a person answers questions or not is up to them. They can follow advice of counsel or not. In this instance, the lawyer said, "I am going to answer the question." His lawyer spoke up: "I am instructing you not to do so." The respondent lawyer went on, "I know what you are instructing me, but I am tired of this whole mess, and I am going to answer the question. Yes, I forged my wife's signature." Wow, what a powerful moment; achieved only because I did not abide by the usual stipulation.

8. Agreeing to waive the sealing and filing of the transcript with the court. Already a standard of practice, transcripts are filed only when necessary for a motion or trial.

The next time you are asked to agree to the usual stipulations, consider the list (and be sure of what the reference is to in your particular jurisdiction) and make a conscious and strategic decision as to those you accept and those you reject. Few agreements have no consequences, even if they are called "usual" in the practice.

Becoming an Expert
on Experts

Taking Effective Expert Witness Depositions

Maybe it's their experience, or perhaps all those articles they have written. Maybe it's the aggressive and confident demeanor with which they express themselves. Whatever the reason, many lawyers experience discomfort when they have to depose an expert witness. There is good reason for this, I suppose; by definition, experts know more about their areas of expertise than we do. And well they should. Isn't that why we've retained them?

Yet the question remains: how do we control the expert in deposition? Is there some way we can gain points even though we do not hold the degrees and experience in medicine, accounting, engineering, or helicopters that the experts have? The answer is a most certain yes.

Lawyers should take comfort in the very fact that we do not share the background and specific training as the expert. If you are looking for some of the poorest examples of a deposition, find a transcript of one taken by a lawyer who does hold the same degrees and even some practical experience in the expert's field. For example, take a lawyer who is a civil engineer who is confident of being able to challenge a civil engineer expert in every way. The transcript will look like a battlefield of insult and innuendo, with wonderful patter that impresses the reader with the question, "I wonder who knows more about civil engineering, the lawyer or the expert?" Unfortunately, the deposition itself is of little value to the development of the lawyer's case theory and strategy. It proves to be little more than a forum for personal challenge.

Rather than a challenge, consider the deposition a means of testing and strengthening your case and theory. The methods are quite simple:

1. Rather than impressing experts with *your* background, challenge experts on the facts that they relied on for their studies.

2. Rather than attacking the credibility of the expert who has been testifying longer than you have been alive, create doubt about the methodology used in this particular case.

3. Rather than permitting experts to maintain control in the deposition because they are asked little more than questions that seek their opinions and basis for opinions, ask the ten questions that experts find difficult to answer.

Experts rely on the facts provided to them by the lawyers who employ them. As such, almost every case has a series of facts that would invalidate or significantly modify the results produced. Use your own expert to help identify the contrary facts that the opposition's expert will want to resist; they will always exist and always provide the basis for an attack.

If an expert is worth his or her reputation, it is unlikely that you will be able to create much discord regarding the expert's character. Rather, look to the methodology employed by that expert. Almost always, an alternative method, if employed, would produce contrary results. Experts will be resistant to such suggestions, but they will have to admit that alternative methods exist. From there, it is a short step toward their recognition that reasonable alternatives can produce equally plausible results.

I began to wonder what questions could trigger discomfort in an expert as he or she sat in the deposition and again at trial. The following ten questions emerged from conversations I have had with experts. I began gathering these questions when an expert sitting next to me on an airplane agreed to share with me the questions that unnerve him at deposition. This expert, of course, had his set responses to the questions, so I share them with you as well. You might as well be ready to challenge the expert, and when you can't intimidate the expert, be able to address the plausible responses you may get.

Q: Tell me about the other side's expert.
A: He (or she) has a fine reputation.
Q: Isn't their expert's opinion as valid as yours?
A: Sure, reasonable minds can differ. I just happen to be right in this case.

Q: Who wrote this document, you or the lawyer?

A: The lawyer, but I reviewed it and agree with the data and conclusions addressed in it.

Q: Assume these contrary facts I presented you. Do they change your opinion in this case?

A: In commentary, the expert on the airplane shared his experience that most facts presented by the lawyers were essentially irrelevant to the analysis. He believed that many lawyers were not properly prepared for the deposition and seemed to be grasping at straws. He agreed that there were probably facts that would produce a contrary result. In such a case, he would respond that these facts were not presented to him or were determined not to be relevant to the analysis. As such, he would be unable to comment without conducting a new analysis, and no one had yet paid him to do so.

Q: Have you ever been wrong?

A: Not when the facts provided me by the lawyer were accurate. In such a case, my analysis is always correct. If the facts or conditions change, then my analysis may change, but it does not mean that I was wrong.

Q: Have you been told not to discuss part of this case?

A: The expert told me that he tells the lawyer, "Don't show me anything you don't want me to consider in an opinion. If I see it, it is fair game."

Q: Are these all the notes you took?

A: This question goes as a warning to an expert who was better off not evaluating the case, because any notes created for the analysis must, of course, be disclosed. Experts are uncomfortable with this question because it presupposes that they did create some sort of discard file. The query is whether any notes deemed not to be relevant to the conclusions were discarded before a final report was drafted. Such behavior would be unethical and inappropriate. As such, experts should warn lawyers, if they see it or write it, it's fair game for discovery. All notes, good and bad, must be integrated into and reflected in the final report.

Q: How much in fees have you received?

A: A common question, it's not difficult to answer. The expert's insight about this question is interesting. He noted that fees (monies collected) are often low. The better question is, "How much have you *invoiced*?" That is where the large numbers can be found. Lawyers, like everybody else, are slow to pay their bills.

Q: In your last session, didn't you testify to the opposite?

A: A good expert will not buy into this, but will require that they review the previous session's transcript before answering. The expert fears that the lawyer will misquote the prior testimony and that he can often explain any confusion upon seeing what was said in the past.

Q: That's not the truth, is it?

A: The expert shared his favorite response: "*I'm* under oath, I must tell the truth, but *you're not*, counsel, are you?" A bit tongue-in-cheek, experts would be ill-advised to respond in a sarcastic or argumentative manner on the stand, but even the underlying point the expert tried to make is wrong. Attorneys are officers of the court, and their behavior is governed by the Rules of Professional Conduct that *require* lawyers to be truthful. There are a lot of other requirements that are aspirational in design, but the requirement to be honest and truthful…that one's required!

Keep these tactics in mind and use your expert to help prepare you to depose the other side's expert. You will find that the pressures are reduced, the task becomes manageable, and the case theory is strengthened.

Lights, Camera, Action!

Taking Effective Video Testimony

I t would be nice to call a casting agency and order the perfect witness for use in a videotape deposition. Unfortunately, our witnesses are who they are, and most people are uncomfortable appearing on video for their deposition or trial testimony.

There are considerations a lawyer should make when deciding whether to put a witness on video, and there are precautions to take when videotape is the chosen alternative for the witness who will be unavailable at trial. In the use of videotape, lawyers are transformed somewhat into directors and producers, deciding what will appear on camera and how the interaction will play out. Unlike written transcripts, there is the added burden and responsibility of a clean production when the visual medium is being used.

First, the lawyer needs to evaluate whether the witness will make a positive impression on videotape. Simply put, some people translate well to tape and others appear to be ill at ease with a camera present; they might actually be more effective giving live testimony. When a witness is deemed to make a poor impression on tape, one very valuable alternative to videotape is still available. Relying on the written transcript, most lawyers will use the services of a paralegal or secretary to read the testimony into the record. The concern is that a reading by someone other than the witness can be even more boring than the testimony by the actual witness. Paralegals and secretaries view their role as merely reading the information into the record. Consider an alternative.

Hire an actor to read the transcript. Consider the value. Although more costly, an actor who looks the part can read the testimony with impact and meaning. Certainly the jury will be instructed that the reader is an actor and is not the actual witness, but odds are that the jurors will nevertheless remember more of the testimony if it is read with effect and impact. Given the option, why not have the information presented effectively rather than as a matter of course? Assuming you would never put an unprepared witness on the stand, the actor fills the gap when a witness will be unavailable and makes a poor appearance on camera. No rules say that a jury must be bored to death by an ineffective colorless stand-in.

If the lawyer decides to proceed with videotaped testimony, then certain considerations must be kept in mind. Use a professional certified videographer who will be responsible for monitoring all microphones and equipment. Things can go on the fritz when you least suspect it, and the professional whose sole job is to monitor the equipment is well worth the cost. The professional videographer can ensure that lighting is sufficient and appropriate and that the background scenery is not distracting, such as a glass wall with a constant parade of people marching back and forth behind the real action.

The witness needs to be prepared for an appearance on camera. Be certain to tell the witness to wear a light gray or blue shirt, rather than white. The color white reflects light on camera and will detract from the witness's appearance. Dark colors, such as navy blue or gray, show up best on camera, and ties or scarves should be dark and plain. It would be unfortunate if effective testimony were clouded by distracting attire.

As the testimony begins, it is essential that the witness address much of the testimony to the camera. This technique is unnatural for most people, because we are accustomed to looking at others eye-to-eye. In this case, the jury will be viewing an image that focuses on the witness, and if the witness is looking at the examiner and not the camera, the jury members will not have a sense that they are being spoken to directly. This skill likely will require significant preparation time by the lawyer and witness as the witness learns to deliver answers into the camera. The lawyer can help the witness along by suggesting, "Tell the ladies and gentlemen of the jury…" This statement can be a useful way to remind the witness to look into the camera.

It is important that everyone be prepared before the video-taping of the deposition. Unlike in written transcripts, rustling papers and other forms of disorganization will be caught on camera, which creates a less-than-desirable image and should be avoided. Keep the table clean and pause the tape if you must, but be certain that the interaction is conducted smoothly and with the appearance of precision.

If graphics or other visuals are used on the tape, be certain that they do not create glare for the camera. If they are covered with protective plastic, for example, they will cause significant glares in the camera when held at less than a ninety-degree angle. The professional videographer will monitor this factor, but the lawyers should be in tune with these types of presentation issues as well.

The videotape is its own record of nonverbal behaviors. As such, lawyers and witnesses must be aware, not only of what they say, but how they say it. Research as far back as the 1920s confirms that our words are less than 10% of the overall message, whereas our voice provides about 40% of the message, and our body carries 55%. Clearly words are important, but the effect and import of those words is more often found in their manner of delivery.

For that reason, it becomes important for the lawyer to monitor volume, rate, and pace. Anger, frustration, and sarcasm don't read on paper but glare as bright as day on videotape. The jury will be provided a great deal of information with which to evaluate the credibility of the witness and the lawyers, most of which will be coming from other factors than the words being spoken. Therefore, rehearsal with the witness and a constant awareness of demeanor on everyone's part is an essential factor for the players on videotape.

Finally, how long should videotape testimony be? Short, with few exceptions. Jurors' attention spans last about fifteen to twenty minutes with a videotape. Longer tapes ensure that the audience will tune out. Much of the reason has to do with the inability to vary the view, angle, and shots of the camera. Americans are accustomed to the MTV version or news footage form of videos, which means the picture changes every seven seconds (really, watch the news or a music video, and you can count off seven seconds; the picture will change by the time you reach seven!). The novelty of "going to the movies" at trial wears off within five minutes, rendering the balance of the testimony a challenge to stay awake. Do whatever it takes to keep the testimony on point, short, and direct. When this is impossible, plan to ask the court for break time, as it is the only alternative to keeping the jury awake.

Videotape is a wonderful addition to the lawyer's arsenal of courtroom tools. Employed without thought and planning, video can be deadly ineffective at trial; used with awareness and an eye toward keeping it interesting, testimony on videotape can be a powerful force in helping guide the jury.

PART IV.

STEPPING INSIDE THE JURORS' MINDS

MEANINGFUL JUROR SELECTION

Trial preparation does not begin the first day of trial. Lawyers have an entire arsenal of research tools available to them so they can truly understand what environment they will encounter when they enter the courtroom and have a strong sense of exactly how they need to present their case to a jury. These tools include the community attitude survey, the focus group, and mock trial.

Taking the Pulse of the Community...Part of the Homework

The Role of Community Attitude Surveys

The community attitude survey is one of the most basic jury consulting tools, but by no means does every case require a study of the prevailing attitudes in the community about a specific issue or concern. Not every client I work with needs such a survey, because some lawyers have significant experience in their communities. When they must make financial trade-offs they may forgo the expense and time involved, because they have a strong sense of the prevailing attitudes and values in the community in which the trial takes place. In addition, lawyers may not need a survey if the issues raised in the case are typical—mainstream—and therefore not expected to trigger any unusual reaction. For the common accident cases and smaller medical malpractice cases, lawyers often look at verdict reports to get a good idea of how juries in a community have responded to similar cases.

For most cases, a community attitude survey is cost prohibitive, but I recall a case in which a socialite wanted one conducted because she wanted to measure her image in the community and how her fellow citizens would react to the drunk-driving charges against her. This woman spent freely only to learn that most jurors were convinced she was guilty. For her, the research revealed that the road ahead was a difficult one; however, she had enough money to investigate the plausibility of various options. The research showed that her status in society worked against her, because the individuals who would be sitting on the jury of her peers believed that people like her would at least try to buy their way out of a legal problem. In a way, our client served as living proof of the research. Ultimately, the woman was convicted, but the reason involved her unwillingness to deal with the reality that her behavior on the videotape taken by the police at the time of the arrest made her condition clear. She could have adopted a strategy that would have made her appear more like common folk, but she seemed unwilling or unable to even try.

When we conduct a community attitude survey, we are thinking about the kinds of jurors that might be predisposed to our client's case, but we also use the information to help us develop a case theme. Developing a theme then helps the lawyers establish direction when they craft their opening statement and closing arguments. The notion of a case theme does not call for voodoo or for creating nonexistent facts, but it does involve searching for just the right analogy or metaphor to help jurors relate to what would otherwise be complicated concepts. In other words, the jury consultant has to work with the client to translate the message into terms that make sense to the layperson.

A community attitude survey is *not* an inexpensive proposition. Even a limited reach into the community to obtain a relevant pulse on the issues of the case will cost in a typical range of $25,000 to $50,000, so two things are important: first, the client must have issues that warrant conducting a community attitude survey, and second, the client must have the resources to fund the research project or have a good reason why one should be done *pro bono*.

Community attitudes may be multi-layered, so a superficial look won't always suffice. The key to a successful community attitude survey is defining the scope and asking the right questions. Scope is important because, like consumer market research, respondents will give up only a few minutes of their time to answer questions during a telephone interview. The more issues we add, the more time it takes, and we then risk more refusals from people who simply will not cooperate longer than a few minutes, especially when they are not compensated for taking part in these surveys.

We need to gather demographic data (age, race, gender, income, etc.) about everyone who answers the attitude survey, because this information provides the framework from which our profiles will emerge for desirable and undesirable jurors. In a criminal case in which the defendant is well known, the lawyers are concerned about community impressions and the venue of the trial. For example, in a case involving allegations of fraud in a relatively complex scheme of financial issues including stock sales, we wanted to learn the extent of the defendant's bad reputation. We knew the defendant—we'll call him Tony—was not an admired man, but my client (his lawyer) wanted to learn if the specific bad impressions of Tony could outweigh the fact that the involved matter was extremely complex. We set out to learn the following about the community:

- What are the prevailing attitudes about Tony?
- Do people remember him from his early days in business? (Tony was a bit of a braggart in his younger days; he announced he was going to put a company out of business and succeeded.)
- Are people familiar with his investments in sports teams?
- What do the people know about buyouts and mergers and financial disclosure?
- What is the community's current impression of his family life? (We knew his nasty divorce would come up in one way or another, not to mention the unexplained death of his first wife.)
- What have the people read and heard about this case?

In order to participate in a community attitude survey, respondents must be qualified, which is a process not unlike a salesperson qualifying a buyer. Participants are qualified through an initial series of questions, once they agree to stay on the phone at all. We ask the questions because we must be certain that these individuals are eligible to sit on a jury, and to ensure that they don't have particular experiences in their background that may automatically disqualify them from being selected for a jury. We also screen for issues that prevent the participant from being fair in the particular case for which the survey is conducted.

We never indicate who is sponsoring the research, so the respondent does not know which side is asking the questions, although they will wonder. We often say we are conducting a research project, making every effort to remove the expectation that the work is actually being done for the trial by a specific party. This is a step away from complete disclosure, but protecting the rights of the party likely outweighs the failure to disclose the case-specific nature of the project. Many people are quite willing to assist scientists who are engaged in research, and independent opinion research is considered scientific.

Next we ask a series of questions to find out the respondent's basic attitudes. The questions depend on whether we want to get a read about prevailing general attitudes in order to see how they might influence a verdict in a case or whether we are after case-specific reactions. It is clear that the prevailing attitudes in a community are critical to the way a case is perceived in that community, which is why lawyers often consider carefully where they will file a lawsuit, given options in filing. For example, a plaintiff has the option of suing for damages in a civil case either where an event, such as an accident, happened, or wherever the defendant resides. Consider just how powerful such a decision can be.

With each community attitude survey conducted, I present my client with the results of the survey report that includes analyses and conclusions. Usually the lawyer is most concerned with the section called "juror profile." Lawyers actually want to know the types of people who are more likely to be favorable to their side, and some lawyers probably rely on this information more than they should. "Yeah, yeah, I see what the community thinks, but who am I after to sit in that jury box?" is the typical question on the mind of the trial lawyer. In reality, no one can predict what one particular human being will do, even though it is based on a profile of similar people. The juror profile can only suggest what any individual might do, yet it is the piece that lawyers find most intriguing.

With the analysis of the community attitude survey data in hand, the lawyers are ready to craft their case theme and theories to fit the types of jurors they hope to reach. This raises the next question, "Will anybody buy our version of what happened in this case?" Answering that question involves using the next tool in the box, the focus group, the setting where the case truly is tested and put together and where argument and evidence meet. In many cases this is the first time the evidence and arguments are subjected to the most powerful test there is, the reaction of a group of non-lawyer laypersons. These individuals will never actually sit on the jury for the case, yet they will have a powerful impact on the way the case is shaped and presented to the real jury.

Adding Certainty to an Uncertain World

Developing Case Strategy with Focus Groups

Have you ever been uncertain how a jury would interpret or react to your case theory or a specific argument? Perhaps you have always assumed that uncertainty is a part of the process with which the trial lawyer must live. The good news is that trial lawyers have available to them pretrial research methods and procedures that test the effectiveness of case theory and can be used to gather feedback on case viability. Pretrial research is invaluable in providing objective insight that in many ways quantifies the odds and bridges the gap between what a lawyer thinks a jury should do and what an actual jury will most likely do at trial. The secret is conducting the research well in advance of the trial so that the conclusions, the points of confusion, and the concerns may be addressed well ahead of the trial date.

One popular form of research that lends insight into the viability of case theory is the focus group. Focus groups provide information about how jury-eligible individuals are likely to respond to your case arguments, specific evidence, and particular case facts. Clearly the information obtained from a focus group is subjective in nature, and in some ways constitutes a healthy brainstorming session. It also reduces uncertainty, as it assists the lawyer during the formative stages of a trial to create arguments on anchor issues.

The method to producing a focus group is as follows: the participants are recruited from the community at large or a similarly situated community. These people should be paid well for their time so that they are willing participants for the day and are also committed to giving their full attention during the rigors of the project. The important point is reaching mock jurors who look like what actual jurors may look like when the actual trial comes, and doing your best to ensure that these mock jurors are not actually on the jury call during the time your trial is to be heard.

The lawyers put arguments together that relate the key issue or issues to be studied. This is not the time to present the entire case, such as in a mock trial, but rather a time to evaluate a particular issue.

The case argument can be presented on videotape or live. From a research perspective, videotape is preferred because several groups can be tested with a guarantee of control over the material. If conducted live, there could likely be a variation in the presentation among subsequent groups. While a live presentation is more interesting to watch than a tape, it is the lawyer's choice to compare and compromise the reliability of the input with the impact of the presentation form. Over the course of several groups, reliability and validity of the data collected should win the consideration. The other value of placing arguments on videotape is the ease of access and analysis that the social scientists (who are likely retained to assist with this research) will have to review and comment on the data, ensuring the proper balance and presentation.

You may be asking, "Wait a minute; are you having us present *both* sides of the case? We present arguments that we anticipate our *opponents* will make at trial?" Exactly. It isn't the same lawyer presenting both sides, but rather two members of the firm who make the presentations. One lawyer plays the part of the other side. This is a critical part of the process. In fact, and I am giving a trade secret away on this one, but it is critical to the trial consultant that we work to be sure that the strongest and most powerful arguments for the *opposing* side are presented to the mock jurors. Truth be told, no one is in a better position to present a strong argument for the other side than are you, because you know your case weaknesses and areas you may have trouble countering at trial. Let's get it all on the table now! It should not surprise you to learn that a successful focus group project occurs when the mock jurors vote *against* my client; that is the circumstance under which most learning takes place. You can't learn much from jurors who think from the outset that you're wonderful and who have nothing bad to say and don't even consider the adverse arguments as plausible.

This is why jury or trial consultants seek to recruit jurors who represent what the actual case jurors might look like, and in fact we really want to find jurors who (through the screening process) we learn are leaning in a direction that is contrary to our client's position. We want to learn as much as possible from these jurors, and you learn more from people who are leaning against your position than from those in favor of it. I hope this makes more sense now. Lawyers who attempt to do this kind of project on their own, but who bring in paralegals and friends to listen to their arguments, are merely presenting to a welcoming audience, one predisposed to agree with that lawyer. There won't be a whole lot of learning happening in that instance.

Back to the process…the participants sit through the presentation of evidence. Prior to the presentations, their attitudes relevant to the case are measured. That is, the participants complete a lengthy attitudinal survey upon arriving at the project, because we need to know the baseline of attitudes and values before any arguments are even presented. Additional attitudinal measurements are taken after the presentation of the plaintiff's case, the defendant's case, and each other phase that may be included in the study, such as rebuttal, and even after the presentation of jury instructions, when those are incorporated as part of the process. In this way, the lawyer is provided not only with the existing attitudes of the mock juror at each phase of the process, but also with the shifts in position and the stability in the strength of those attitudes as the process proceeds.

Following the presentation of the evidence and the taking of the requisite measures, the mock jury can be permitted to deliberate. This process should be recorded on videotape for later analysis, but in the meantime, a wealth of information is being gathered as the participants discuss and evaluate the evidence and arguments presented to them through the course of the project. This deliberation will assist in highlighting what evidence was not presented (perhaps because it does not exist) that was perceived to be necessary for the jury to find in one direction or the other. In addition, comments on lawyer style and presentation are gathered that can be invaluable to the lawyers who seek to establish a credible and strong presence in front of the jury.

Finally, the lawyers (or, preferably, the social scientists retained for the project) meet with the jurors to gather additional information on the underlying and guiding processes. Questions regarding lawyer skill, approach, strength of arguments, inconsistencies in story, and anything else of concern and interest can be asked of the jury in a guided and structured fashion. In this way, issues left unclear at the end of deliberation are not left to uncertainty. The researcher confirms, tests, and pins down the key issues and points.

Ultimately, the results of the research are written up by the researcher for presentation to the lawyer. This report includes not only a summary of the data gathered but also an evaluation of trends and a series of suggestions on directions for the future of the case. It is easy to see the importance of conducting such research relatively early in the development of case theory while there is still sufficient time to make changes and gather additional information through remaining discovery efforts.

My company, Decision Analysis, has developed an interesting variation of the traditional focus group model. We have our clients make their presentations, but we stay in the room and are prepared to interrupt and stop them at a moment's notice. We'll stop the presentation to go to the mock jurors at that moment and get feedback. Does the argument make sense? Is it confusing? What do you need to hear to counter this argument? This approach helps us isolate specific arguments and statements so we can dissect them on the spot. It's a powerful technique that sheds significant light on the pieces of a case theory or argument. You can learn more about the work of our research group at www.decision-analysis.com.

Focus groups can also be used to evaluate the anticipated theories of your adversary. For example, if a liquidated damages theory turns out to be obscure and uncompelling to the potential jurors, the party's settlement posture and trial theory can be dramatically affected. Ultimately, the gathered data is used to help determine whether changes in case strategy are necessary prior to trial, whether settlement should be explored because of an overall weak case, or whether a case is strong in its present form.

The value of quantitative testing in a case is to explore the significance of patterns observed in the data. The first level of significance testing can indicate whether a specific response pattern reflects a chance difference or a real difference. For example, if 55% of the test jurors find negligence while 45% make no such finding, significance testing will show whether that difference is merely a matter of chance or whether it is a useful indicator of probability in other, similar situations. Quantitative analysis can also calculate a frequency distribution of likely award amounts and estimate the probability that a damage award made by a similar jury will fall within a specified range of dollar amounts. In short, this research can add a sense of certainty to what is, by definition, an uncertain jury deliberation process. Finally, this research can help determine the extent to which damage awards may be a function of the strength of juror opinions on a particular issue.

For years, some lawyers were wary of the assistance offered by social science to adding certainty in the courtroom. In reality, growing efforts toward swifter case resolution can be facilitated by learning earlier, and with some certainty, the likely direction your case will take. For the well-prepared lawyer, it offers another and quite significant level of input and analysis to be used in successful litigation.

It's Not What You Are but How You Live

The Role of Demographics in Jury Selection

Whenever I appear as a jury expert on television regarding that week's "Case of the Century," or whenever I give a newspaper interview regarding jury profile in a case, the anchor or writer always has the same question: "Demographically, what does each side want on the jury?" No matter how much I tell them that demographics do not play the critical role in that determination, the question is always asked, and I find myself having to talk about whether women or men, whites or African Americans, young or old, are what the lawyers want on the jury. But I get it; Matt Lauer, Anderson Cooper, Paula Todd, and all the rest have good television to create, so as a good and compliant guest I must play along. Underlying the inquiry of what jurors are desired is an assumption that a single demographic factor can determine the jury selection decisions. In reality, research does not support this assumption.

For many trial lawyers, a desire to select or reject jurors on the basis of gut or internal feelings often outweighs any scientific study or conclusions regarding demographic factors as an aid to juror evaluation. Yet most lawyers do consider the specific demographic variables of jurors, which include gender, race, nationality, and socioeconomic status. While complete reliance on juror demographics is not possible or desirable, the sophisticated insight potentially provided by such evaluation can offer significant data for the trial lawyer's consideration. The error lies in believing that any one factor will be determinative of what a juror will do.

Most lawyers wouldn't mind a complete clinical assessment of each potential juror with an opportunity to probe deeply into juror attitudes, but reality requires otherwise. There simply isn't time to pursue that depth of analysis. (Wouldn't it be great to have each prospective juror lie on a couch for a few hours as we ask our in-depth questions?) In federal courts and in many state jurisdictions, jury picks are being made based on inquiry solely from the bench.

Of course, another side to this issue is that there appears to be an inherent intellectual bias against using demographics as a tool of jury selection. We have, to a great degree, become predisposed to accepting as fact that gender, age, ethnicity, and other similar characteristics are simply too crude to be predictive of complex juror behavior.

Modern trial lawyers have moved well beyond a historic and all-too-strong reliance on oral tradition to decide who shall serve on a jury. Have seasoned lawyers yet forgotten the now famous rules for jury selection from a criminal defense perspective well established by Clarence Darrow? A walk down memory lane will remind you that some of Darrow's famous rules included the following: Irishmen are ideal because they are emotional, kindly, and sympathetic; Presbyterians are cold as the grave and know right from wrong, but seldom find anything right, so get rid of them before they contaminate the others; and be certain to choose a person who laughs. Darrow noted that a juror who laughs hates to find *anyone* guilty. Rare is the lawyer who, today, does not cringe upon considering these outrageous, yet largely demographic, jury-selection strategies. I am sure they worked on some level for the great Darrow, but I also believe something more and something deeper was going on in his mind.

Those lawyers who hold a bias against demographics are not without foundation to their positions. Demographics have historically performed rather poorly in social-science models. The problem, however, likely lies not in the characteristics themselves, but in how social scientists have looked at them in the past.

Moreover, demographic characteristics have changed through a merger of what were considered significant differences between the sexes. This finding, however, does not render gender to be an insignificant factor for jury section; the distinctions have changed over time in the areas of racial, ethnic, or social characteristics. Communities have become, by and large, more diverse and integrated than in the past.

A case study conducted by Trial Behavior Consulting Inc. in San Francisco illustrates the need for lawyers to rely somewhat on surface characteristics to assist in jury selection.[7] The key to effective selection, however, is discerning the subtle patterns that lie beneath the more obvious features of the jury profile. In the study of a particular case analysis, gender was not shown to be a factor in that case. Neither was ethnicity in that case.

While some differences in jurors' dispositions were found, none of them was statistically significant in the case. Upon integrating the factors, however (in the case studied, gender and ethnicity), a significant finding emerged, which indicated jurors who were more likely to vote pro-plaintiff. Absent a consideration of the integration of factors, the leaning of the particular combination of factors became evident.

Therefore, in most cases it is unlikely that any single factor will determine what a juror will do; however, every expectation clearly has exceptions. Lawyers can benefit from considering the integration of demographic factors. In fact, the more factors integrated into the equation, the greater the predictability level.

Research indicates that beyond any specific demographic factor, a juror's decision-making process is affected by his or her life experiences. Uncovering these experiences sheds light on the influence of particular demographics for that person. For example, growing up in a particular race or nationality will potentially lead to different verdict votes depending on whether that person grew up poor or wealthy, as part of a broken family, and a host of other life experiences.

It is wise to take caution in any regard against selecting or rejecting jurors based solely on demographics. For one thing, if

7 Lisnek and Beaton. "Can You Judge a Jury by Its Cover?"

the story or continuity being presented in the trial is less than consistent, coherent, and complete, then the jurors may likely be less affected by their own demographic makeup than they are following the law as it is related to them. Encouraged to not set aside the common affairs of life but to utilize them in the deliberation process, it is easy to see how demographics are a two-edged sword.

Beyond demographics, juror decision making is affected by life experiences, group dynamics, and group interaction. That is to say that jury decision making will be affected by the way in which the jurors interact with each other in the deliberation room. So much for making decisions based only on one's gender or race!

The likely future of Supreme Court rulings offers an irony: my crystal ball foresees an expanding effort by the conservative court to further limit lawyer freedom in the exercise of peremptories as more and more protected categories become a basis upon which lawyers cannot systematically remove jurors. The good news: research makes it clear that the single-factor approach as the jury selection criteria will provide faulty results.

In one respect, the factors and life experiences of a juror help us understand how a juror is likely to view the evidence, but those same factors very may well lead the juror to take a step in the unanticipated direction if that juror finds the party's story to be contradictory to the direction of the evidence. Put differently, all the demographic factors in the world can't overcome a weak case story, which means that case preparation still stands as the single most important factor that needs to be under control before stepping into the courtroom.

Once Upon a Time...

Storytelling at Trial

There are three sides to every story: your client's, the other party's, and of course the truth. Most lawyers recognize that the truth lies somewhere between all the versions of events recounted after the fact.

It is not that everyone or anyone involved is lying, necessarily, but rather it is a reflection of the natural process called slippage. Over time, certain details of our experiences get lost from memory, while others get reshaped within our minds.

Clients will, by definition, delete details from the first retelling of events forward. The impact of this point for the courtroom presentation is that lawyers need to recognize that they will not be *re-creating anything* in the courtroom; rather, the lawyer's role is to create a new reality, one that is consistent, complete, appealing, and, ultimately, compelling in the jury's eyes. The process begins in the client interview, extends through depositions and other discovery, and must be established without flaw at trial.

The jury will compare the competing accounts as it attempts to sort out the truth from the confusion of the testimony and evidence presented to them. Their decision will emerge from consideration of what I call the "case continuity" or "account" presented by each side.

W. Lance Bennett and Martha S. Feldman's storytelling model explains how jurors connect evidence to produce a verdict.[8] The model presents a framework for understanding the manner in which juries process information.

The terms case continuity and account are better suited to the relating of events at trial. "Story" suggests creation of something that is not true; it is wise to seek a sense of reality and realism. The trial lawyer's mind-set from the point of the client interview forward needs to establish a continuity that is real and believable. Clearly, what is presented in the courtroom is not a retelling of reality; the trial is too far removed from past events for this to be the case. More accurately, trial testimony retells events based on past experience.

The Bennett and Feldman model and others like it view the story/continuity as the organizer of information that enables the jurors to perform two interpretive operations: first, locate

8 Bennett and Feldman. *Reconstructing Reality in the Courtroom.* (William C. Brown Company Publishers, 1981).

the central action in the case; and second, construct the most credible inferences among the bits of information presented through testimony and evidence. Jurors seek a way in their own minds and through their deliberation to explain events that are in dispute. The only way to do so is to compare and contrast the accounts presented.

At each phase of the process, jurors look for a connection among the elements of testimony presented. In effect, the jurors consider whether a set of events *could have* occurred the way in which the lawyers and the evidence suggest.

The first step in developing the story is for the lawyer to isolate the central action around which the story develops and to which all parties agree. The central action is the glue that frames the continuity and keeps circumstances in context. It becomes the gauge for inconsistency and a tool for evaluating circumstantial evidence.

For example, imagine that the following information is presented through testimony at trial: A plaintiff is injured while using a tool manufactured by the NeverFail tool company to perform simple carpentry jobs around his house. He had used a similar tool once before and claims to have read the instructions before using this tool. As a result of the incident, he can no longer work or perform daily functions.

Certain surface-level inferences may be made from the testimony: The plaintiff cut his hand while using NeverFail's dangerous product, and, as a result, the plaintiff has experienced and continues to experience pain, suffering, and financial loss. The central action, or what specifically caused the plaintiff's injury and what the defendant could have done to avoid it, is unclear.

If the plaintiff fails to establish each of the story elements, he will likely fail to meet his burden of proving all of the elements of the cause of action. For instance, in the example the plaintiff fails to explain and establish that the manufacturer defendant breached its duty of care to the plaintiff as a user of the equipment. An adjustment of facts can quickly shift the evaluation.

Suppose that the jury learns that the NeverFail tool has a safety guard that has been known to snap off while the product is working, and that this blade guard was missing from the product after the plaintiff was injured. By establishing the central action—namely, that the plaintiff's injury was caused by a flaw in the defendant's product, of which the manufacturer had notice—the story becomes more complete. The modified version of the story comes closer to meeting the plaintiff's burden of proof than the previous version.

The defendant may counter the plaintiff's continuity by challenging whether he established a cause of action for negligence, or the defendant may show that the plaintiff's testimony can be interpreted differently.

For instance, the defendant's expert testifies that the safety guard was designed and working properly but that the plaintiff misused it. The defendant might show that its product's safety guard had never injured anyone before, that the plaintiff was intoxicated when he used the product, and that the plaintiff was not using the product for its intended purpose.

The jury is then left to weigh two potentially credible accounts to determine what really happened. How the defendant selects the strategy to employ often depends on the strength and completeness of each account.

Lawyers can determine the strength of the adversary's competing account by determining the strength of their own client's account. Opposing counsel will certainly seek to uncover the inconsistencies in the adversary's account. Thus each lawyer needs to anticipate and prepare for any counter accounts.

The storytelling model is not without its limitations. It fails to seriously consider the effect and impact of witness and lawyer credibility and the resulting impressions on jurors. Ultimately, research suggests that the verdict is more likely to side with the more complete and consistent account that also is related through credible sources. The model also assumes that jurors will appropriately connect the testimony to the central action.

Beyond the commonly accepted need for a trial theme, case continuity is the real guide for measuring case potential and the likely verdict.

Reality Is Just a Myth

How Jurors Process Information

Few lawyers claim to have total comfort when they are selecting a jury. Some lawyers know a good juror when they see one; others know them when they hear the answers to questions; and some get a sense in their gut that guides their decisions. In reality, how can we really know whether a juror is telling the truth or just relating answers that are socially appropriate? After all, let's remember that the process that we call jury selection is in reality a process of de-selection. Lawyers do not get to keep the jurors they like on the jury; rather they must remove the jurors who they believe will not be good jurors for them. With both sides doing the same thing, the jury theoretically ends up with jurors who do not hold extreme views on either end of the spectrum, but rather are open to either and both sides of the case. Reality doesn't quite back up this conclusion, but the goal and point are well taken.

We can make a dent in our inability to read veracity of jurors by stepping a bit further into the minds of those prospective jurors. The trial lawyer's task is to determine and evaluate the manner in which prospective jurors think and process information. Knowing this, the trial lawyer can formulate questions that better align with the reality of each juror. Understanding this process produces the most powerful insight available to trial lawyers today.

The process of communication and the science of neuro-linguistic programming (NLP) rely primarily on our senses: sight, hearing, and sensation (smell, taste, and touch). Each of us uses the three processing modes at various times, but we each carry a preference for one of them. Your goal in voir dire is to identify the means by which particular jurors prefer to process testimony and then modify your inquiries accordingly.

Applicable to clients and colleagues, we can focus the analysis on how jurors process information.[9] For example, many jurors will be primarily *visual* processors. Their minds work like a View-Master, transforming input into pictures for interpretation. For example, when vision-based people describe events in which they were involved, they relate events by describing the pictures that fly through their minds. Your questions for voir dire should guide that juror toward retrieving visual information.

---

9   Lisnek and Oliver. *Communication Power: Communication Strategies for Trial Lawyers.* (PESI Law Publications, 2001).

Other people prefer naturally to think and process information in *words or sounds*. These hearing-based (auditory) people have a constant discussion going on in their heads; they react primarily to the sounds or voices that occupy their minds. They listen both to and for details and can locate the logical connections between ideas. Asking them to envision a scene or feel emotions presents these jurors with difficulty. Your questions should guide them to process auditory information.

People who think in terms of feelings operate on an *emotional* level, rather than responding to what they see or hear. They rely on gut reactions and feelings. People who think this way convert external information into a feeling, then sense the feeling, and finally transform their feelings into terms they can communicate.

People provide clues as to how they are thinking at any given point in time, so we as lawyers need to learn how to tap into them. These indicators include posture, gestures, breathing, and many others. The easiest of all the indicators to describe are the words selected by the jurors and the ways in which they move their eyes.

You can start testing and experimenting with this material today. Vision-oriented people use visual words, including "clear," "picture," "focus," "see," and "foggy." They use phrases such as, "I see what you mean," "Picture this for a moment," "In my view," "Imagine, if you will," "Don't look so blue in the face," "He has a dark personality," and "He appears so transparent."

When asked a question, a vision-based juror will flick the eyes up and to the right or left to find the answer. While eye movement may not be exaggerated, a subtle upward shift of the eye indicates a search for a visual answer. For right-handed persons, looking up and to the right means that they are constructing a visual image. If they look up and to the left, they are remembering a visual image. Periodically persons will create visual images by staring straight ahead and dramatically de-focusing their eyes. The eye movement of a left-handed person, or more accurately a right-brain-dominant person, runs opposite for creating and remembering information.

Hearing-oriented jurors select sound-based words to describe what is happening in their minds. They select words like "hear," "listen," "say," "talk," and "rings." They will use phrases such as, "I hear what you mean," "That sounds good to me," "That rings a bell," "Talk to me for a minute," "I want you to explain," "That clicks for me," and "Everyone is clamoring for my attention." Note the differences from a visual-based speaker.

Hearing-based persons move their eyes from side to side. Right-handed persons looking to their right are indicating that they are constructing or creating a sound. Looking to their left means they are remembering a sound. The opposite is true for left-handed, or, more accurately, right-brain-dominant persons.

Feeling-based persons select tactile words, which include "comfort," "feel," "grasp," and "handle." They use phrases such as "I'm uncomfortable with…" "I want to grasp this situation," "There's a hot idea," "I just don't feel that…" and "That kind of talk is hard to handle."

Kinesthetic, or feeling, based persons look down and to the left (opposite for left-handed, right-brain-dominant folks) to access feelings. These downward glances are often subtle. For example, clients asked how they feel about something will look up to visualize the situation and then downward to get in touch with the feelings related to the mental picture created.

Keep notes on the words, phrases, and eye movements of jurors during voir dire. Structure your questions to permit the juror to process in a way most comfortable for him or her. Ask a vision-based juror to "describe" experiences, a hearing-based juror to "tell about..." their experiences, and a feeling-based juror for their "sense of..." their experiences. Observe eye movements as you ask for known factual information (address and employment, for example) to test for consistency. Once you have an indication or gather a sense (so to speak) about jurors, you can explore relevant attitudes and observe how they access and report information.

Trial lawyers who understand juror information processing will create better voir dire questions; i.e., questions that better align with the juror's preferred processing mode. The result is control over voir dire interaction and insight into the creation and structuring of opening statements, closing arguments, and witness examinations.

Because jurors need information related in the way they most easily process it, lawyers must accept the burden to present a balance among all three processing modes to ensure that each juror gets what he or she seeks. It isn't how *we* process information that matters, but how the jurors process information that should guide the way in which we put our presentation together.

The Magic of
the Mirror

Building Nonverbal Rapport with Jurors

Rapport is not the lawyer's *goal* with jurors in courtroom interaction; rather it is a footprint or result of a natural process called matching and mirroring, which occurs between most human beings who are indeed in rapport. This concept presents a significant shift in our efforts to seek out intent and purpose from jurors and clients. In fact, building rapport with jurors is behavior based. Human beings *act first* and provide explanations later, to be blunt about it.[10] Think about your client's explanations for his

---

10   Lisnek and Oliver. *Courtroom Power: Communication Strategies for Trial Lawyers.* (PESI Law Publications, 2001).

or her own actions. Most lawyers have little difficulty knowing that others, including the adversarial party, will have alternate explanations for the same behaviors. Humans, as intelligent primates, can always explain their behavior and do so in many different ways if we need to.

Rapport, or the commonality and alignment between lawyers and jurors, is grounded in conduct, not interpretations. The more behaviors we have in common with another person, the greater the likelihood for rapport to develop and thrive. As a rule, people are comfortable with others who act similarly to themselves. This is the evidence of and for rapport. Behavioral differences between lawyers and jurors suggest an *absence* of rapport. With awareness and some training in behavioral cues, lawyers can build rapport both consciously and subconsciously with jurors and clients.

Creating rapport with a jury as a whole is not an easy task. It is nearly impossible for lawyers to find any one behavior that will be shared with every juror. Focusing in on one commonality that is shared with one juror does not mean that rapport will be created with others for whom that behavior is not a part of their natural functioning.

Lawyers and many other people typically think that rapport is created through language. For example, if jurors act as though they are hot and the lawyer believes the courtroom is muggy, the lawyer mentions the condition to the judge or, if the jurors appear disturbed by external noise, the lawyer once again raises the issue in the hope of establishing rapport. The flaw is the lawyer's assumption or interpretation about the jurors' behavior. Because explanation and intent merely follow behavior, though, there are many more equally compelling explanations for that same behavior. Does discomfort not look like frustration? The best the lawyer can do under this behavioral theory is to present similar behavioral cues and put the search for juror meaning aside.

Simply put, "Why?" is an irrelevant inquiry about human behavior; it produces only fabrication (or hallucination, for the visual folks) and post-behavior explanation. There are always more explanations to be uncovered for any particular behavior. Perhaps the point is best illustrated through this all-too-real example: remember the juror who smiled and nodded in the affirmative toward you throughout the entire trial? You assumed that particular juror was on your side; the cues seemed clear enough, but then that juror turned out to be the one leading the charge to hang your client out to dry!

What went wrong? When did that juror turn against you? Under the behavioral theory, the answer is quite simple. You were never able to rely on your interpretation of that juror's behavior in the first place. There were several other explanations for that same behavior, such as the juror's unconscious internal confirmation that your case affirmed his or her initial distaste for your case, so those nods were actually cues of your defeat. The interpretations were irrelevant. Only the *juror's* behavior mattered, and it was consistent. You just muddied the waters with the application of interpretation and imposed meaning.

How do we know what a juror's behavior means? Answer: We don't. Can we ever understand when a juror is in agreement with us, or not? Answer: Yes. Every person has his or her own cues for agreement and rejection. The cues vary from person to person, but each person will always use the same cues to signal agreement or disagreement. Lawyers need to learn what each juror's cues are for agreement and disagreement. We learn this information by asking simple yes or no questions at the start of voir dire. Carefully observe the juror's nonverbal cues, as minute as they may be, and learn them, because they will be the same cues used every time that juror agrees or disagrees, at trial and in every other setting.

The challenge is learning what to look for and how to monitor it. The good news is that lawyers can be trained in the skill. Once lawyers learn and understand each juror's cues, they can monitor where each juror is with relation to the case.[11]

In addition to understanding each juror's agreement cues, lawyers can work to develop rapport on an other-than-conscious level. This is not as difficult as it may seem, because much of what it takes is natural to all human primates.[12]

Subconscious rapport develops through the appropriate use of mirroring and matching of gestures, vocal tone, and word-type selection. This conduct creates sameness between lawyer and juror. The technique of mirroring and matching operates at the subconscious level, because it occurs naturally. It can be a conscious tool of the effective communicator. Humans will automatically follow and mirror the behaviors of others. Just observe the position of the person next to you on the airplane; as a rule, that behavior is just like yours. Lawyers can consciously match body positions, vocal cues, and thinking process.

Subtly matching the body position of persons as they sit in a chair is an extremely effective way of initiating a subconscious level of rapport. Effective communicators will also match the level of tension in the other person's body and the other person's breathing rate, both of which establish a subconscious

11 Lisnek and Oliver. *Courtroom Power.* (PESI Law Publications, 2001).
12 Ibid.

bond of rapport. Matching breathing rate further accentuates the same sensations in physiology that the juror creates.

The lawyer can also match vocal tone, pitch, volume, and speed. A person who speaks loudly is most comfortable with someone else who speaks loudly. If a lawyer speaks very slowly and the juror speaks very quickly, all will experience discomfort with the dissimilarity. The master communicator matches voice, delivery, and language style of others and remembers these components of speech are nearly 40% of the impact of our message.

To test for rapport: 1) carefully observe each juror's posture, body position, vocal tone, and breathing rate; 2) match the cues and observe the mirroring that naturally occurs anyway within ten to fifty seconds; and 3) if the person mirrors back the new behavior, the lawyer will know that rapport has been established. If the person does not mirror back the shift, this is behavioral evidence that rapport does not yet exist.

Let's not underestimate the power of matching and mirroring language itself, not just using body position, gestures, and paralinguistic cues, but we can also create rapport through a matching of words, terms, and phrases. For example, when a juror says on voir dire that he was "ripped off," I remind my clients to pay attention to that phrase and perhaps work it into their opening or closing where appropriate and to be sure and look at that juror when they use the phrase. The interesting point here is that most people have words and phrases they use all the time that others associate with them, but that they are actually unaware of themselves. If your friends mock you for saying a certain turn of phrase, it is not matching and mirroring; it is mocking and a wasted opportunity to build rapport with you.

One of my favorite examples was a young associate who told me that the partner of the firm to whom he reported always came into his office about 8:00 at night as he readied to leave his office and head home. The partner would drop a new file in his inbox and say, "Here's a new learning opportunity for you!" It drove him crazy. He just wanted to get out; it was late, and in comes a new "learning opportunity?" He could not care less. I asked him whether that partner used the phrase knowingly. He said no, that it just seemed a natural turn of phrase for her, so my suggestion emerged. He was due for his annual review only a few weeks away from when he told me this story. I encouraged him to go into that review, and when asked how things were going, to respond, "Ya know, as I think back over the *learning opportunities* I've had over the past few months, I realize how much I have grown as a lawyer and a professional." The point is that he could mock that phrase and suffer the consequences; he could ignore the phrase and put things in his own terms; or, by using the phrase as his boss would use it, he could build a connection to her in her own world, and the power of such a connection cannot be underestimated.

Experiment with this idea in your own interactions. When someone uses a word or phrase that catches your ear, use it back with him or her in a way that *that person* would use it. Watch the positive reaction of the other person and the increase in rapport. People like people who are like themselves, and using the words the other person uses in the way that the other person uses them is one of the easiest and most powerful ways to see rapport building in action.

In a significant shift in our thinking regarding human interaction, explanations and interpretations are found to *follow* behavior, not precede it. Humans will do what humans do naturally, so there is little need to search for meaning. The challenge and opportunity for lawyers lies in identifying the behavioral cues that each person uses to indicate where the person stands in relation to the lawyer and witnesses who seek to establish this thing called rapport.

Lawyers create reality in the courtroom. They shape the evidence in such a way as to guide the perception of that evidence in the minds of the jurors—if they do it right! The next series of articles explores the tools that shape reality. Because many people find the idea that lawyers can create or reshape reality to be either awesome or hard to believe, I begin with a look at the People v. Philip Spector *case, where a jury could not reach a decision that public opinion and television commentators seemed to find an easy one to reach. How does that happen? Where is reality?*

From Wall of Sound to Jailhouse Rocks

Reframing Reality: A Look Back at
People v. Philip Spector

People are always astounded when a jury verdict comes in that does not reflect what they expected it to be from their following of media accounts. Look no further than O. J. Simpson's murder trial, Robert Blake, Michael Jackson, and Phil Spector, and you know exactly what I am talking about. My office worked in the Simpson and Spector cases, so I experienced that public reaction in a direct way. What I know, though, and if you are a trial lawyer, what you know as well, is that the trial people follow in the newspapers is not the trial that is going on inside the courtroom. Laypersons often ask, "What is wrong with the judicial system? That guy did it!" Again, they don't understand the power of burden of proof or the fact that the newspapers likely are reporting much information that is never admitted into evidence for a jury to consider. Beyond this simplistic point, though, we can go deeper for explanation and understanding, and that takes me into a concept known as reframing.

How is it that we can explain a jury verdict that appears to be at odds with reality? Can the difference between a jury's verdict and the public's perceived reality be more than a reflection of the way evidence was put into context for the jury? The power of framing and reframing meaning may lie well beyond the more simple strategic decisions lawyers make in every case. To explain this concept, I will use the *People v. Philip Spector* murder case. Recall that legendary music producer Phil Spector was charged with murder in the death of actress Lana Clarkson. The two met in a restaurant one evening, Ms. Clarkson went back to Mr. Spector's home (known as "the Castle"), and hours later was found dead in a chair, the result of a gunshot fired in her mouth. Was it murder? Was it an accident? Or was it a suicide? The facts as they were presented led the public to think it had to be a murder. Spector was known for pulling guns out and pointing and threatening women he was dating, Clarkson had a great deal of alcohol in her system, and it just seemed inviting to believe that the two argued, perhaps Ms. Clarkson tried to leave, and one way or another Spector pulled the trigger. It didn't help his case that a limo driver who waited outside his home testified that Spector walked out of the home, gun in hand, and allegedly said, "I think I killed somebody."

Yet forensic science told a very different story. The upward angle of the gun in Clarkson's mouth when it went off made it quite unlikely, if not impossible, that Spector could have been at the required angle with the gun in his hand. In addition, Spector was apparently wearing a white dinner jacket that should have been drenched with blood spatter in the wake of a gun shot only inches away, and yet the coat exhibited very little spatter on it at all. Other forensic evidence suggested his fingertips could not have been closer than two to six feet to her mouth at the time of the shooting, based on the spatter evidence. And oh, yes, the limo driver's first language was not English, but Portuguese, and the phrase the driver recalled hearing, when translated from or to Portuguese, is very close to something different, such as, "I think Somebody has been killed," a distinction of significant importance. And while Spector may have liked to have held a gun, he never shot at any one.

The jury hanged in the case, unable to come to a unanimous verdict. In the end, and following a change in jury instructions that would have eased the way to a conviction, there were two jurors who could not be convinced that the prosecution had met its burden of proof. I greatly simplified this case just to establish a framework to discuss reframing. And it should be noted that in the retrial of the case, Spector was found guilty of murder. Why? There were many differences from the first trial to the second, including a change in defense lawyers, a shift in case strategy and story, less involvement of the jury consultants, and the ultimate selection of the second jury. Most relevant and powerful was the difference in the way issues were framed in the second trial. These are the strategic calls of the legal team as they review and compile the evidence to be presented.

The function of reframing is to recognize that every behavior is useful in some context. For example, everyone would agree that the act of murder is wrong, but stripped of its intent and context (part of the reframing effort), the conduct involved in murder is reduced down to a basic act—killing. Removed from the context of murder, killing can occur in a variety of settings, including suicide, which was one of the possibilities raised by the Spector defense and supported by much evidence that Ms. Clarkson was very depressed at her inability to ignite her movie career and talked and wrote to friends of a desire to kill herself as a result. Of course, others testified she would never consider such a thing, but that's what makes trials fascinating events. Killing could also be accidental, which reflects a very different mind-set than murder, to be sure.

The next step in reframing is to ask: Is there ever a time when this basic act of killing is acceptable? Many people would acknowledge self-defense or even war (in theory, anyway) as acceptable contexts for the act of killing.

To provide another but powerful example, rape is an act everyone considers to be wrong; but stripped of its intent, force, and the other clearly unacceptable components, the basic act involved is reduced to sexual intercourse. Most people would view this basic conduct to be appropriate in some contexts, such as procreation and to exhibit love for another.

In short, meaning is created in context; put differently, there is no meaning without its context. Think about it; take the baggage away from any conduct, and it can be made acceptable in some context. It is not any particular behavior, but the context in which it occurs that determines its meaning. This is not necessarily an easy concept to get a handle on, but as a communication strategy, it is incredibly powerful.

It is human nature to accept or challenge the frame offered, rather than change it, yet if meaning and context are connected, what we really need to do to change meaning is to break the connection between the act and the context. In other words, take the conduct at issue and place it in a *different* context that permits the jury to respond differently. Reframing means generalizing a behavior until a positive meaning emerges or can be uncovered in some context. Intercourse in the setting called rape is wrong and punishable; intercourse between two consenting adults should trigger a different and more positive reaction.

To reframe a behavior, ask, "What is the *intent* of this behavior?" In the Spector case, if a juror considered what the intent of Spector's killing Clarkson would be, they may have considered the possibilities of his wanting to keep her from leaving or punishing her, perhaps, for not performing sexually with him. Are these powerful intents? Do they support a theory underlying killing when Spector had never before actually pulled a trigger of any gun on anyone? If you considered whether Clarkson chose to kill herself in the setting of Spector's home, what would her intent be? Taking a step she long considered taking to finally end the professional and now emotional suffering of a failed career? Perhaps mixed with alcohol, any common sense and reason get pushed aside, and offered a gun and the chance to take the ultimate step, Clarkson decided to do just that and end it all. This is the essence of reframing; considering intent and then exploring the alternatives to an intent that may better explain an act or behavior. Reframing takes the next and final step of confirming that this event, the one at trial, is one of those times that the alternate meaning, the reframe, is what happened.

Reframing is an extremely powerful technique. It can dissect perceived cause-effect relationships and shift their meaning. It can add uncertainty where there once was certainty. For the lawyer, it is the most powerful tool available, because when the technique works successfully, jurors not only act in accordance with the reframing but also believe with all their heads and hearts in the truth of the reframed meaning. In *Spector*, it may very well be that many jurors looked at the story component and found it more likely than not that he killed her, rather than she killed herself, but criminal trials are not decided on what feels right or what makes more sense. They are decided on the prosecution's meeting its burden of proof beyond a reasonable doubt. Without forensic evidence and motive strongly supporting an intentional act on the part of Spector, some jurors found they could not convict. The defense presented a powerful response to the prosecution's theory; it may have seemed possible that Spector killed Clarkson, but it was just as possible for some jurors that something else happened that night.

Reality lies in the uninterrupted showing of continuous movements. If the prosecution could present a story that placed a gun in Spector's hand, blood spatter all over his white jacket and his body, and other factors, the reframe may not have worked, but jurors couldn't get from A to Z on the prosecution's telling of the story. They couldn't place the gun in Spector's hand, couldn't put his hand at close range to Clarkson's mouth, couldn't place Spector close enough to pull that trigger. How can you convict someone just because your gut may suggest that he or she did a particular and specific act? When someone's life and freedom are on the line, you as juror best apply the burden of proof carefully and completely.

Consider the mountain of evidence the prosecution had against O. J. Simpson in his murder trial that led the public at large to believe it was an open-and-shut case, but that led to an acquittal by the jury after only a few hours of deliberation. The infamous Bronco chase was described as a flight from justice by the prosecution, but the defense reframed it as a ride triggered by base fear and grief, because Simpson knew he would be charged with a crime he had not committed. Blood evidence (society's introduction to DNA) so powerfully presented as certain proof of guilt was challenged by the defense as either being tainted or planted in a conspiracy by the police.

Reframing is powerful indeed. For current or future cases covered by the media, consider how reframing works. Was former Illinois Governor Rod Blagojevich taking money for President Obama's former senate seat or was this nothing more than politics as usual? His corruption trial will explore that distinction. Did Casey Anthony really murder her own child, Caylee? Or was she a loving mother who didn't know what to do when faced with a missing child and feared police would come to the wrong conclusion? Did Drew Peterson really murder his third wife, Kathleen Savio, by drowning her in a bathtub given that the coroner originally called the death accidental? Every day, another event, another case, and another trial. Every case, lawyers on both sides doing their job to prove their client should prevail.

Pay close attention to how each side provides contradictory but very separate meaning for underlying intent by the actors in the case, and you'll gain a better understanding of how verdicts can sometimes conflict with public perception and expectation and also highlight the very powerful art of lawyering found in the ability to reframe meaning for a jury.

Life Is Like…

The Power of Metaphors in Voir Dire, Opening, and Closing the Case

Every lawyer would like to know what issues are important to potential jurors, yet our ability to ask questions of jurors is often limited, or in the case of federal court, nearly nonexistent. There are clues available to us that go beyond the words prospective jurors speak, which may be indicative of their personal attitudes and values.

In short, the clues exist in the "life metaphors" that jurors, and all of us, for that matter, wear (sometimes literally) on our sleeve. The technique described here emerges from the concepts and theory of Charles Faulkner.[13]

Meaningful life metaphors of jurors are illustrated by their answers, but when answers are limited, they may be visible through the icons they exhibit through clothing. Have you paid attention to the pins, jewelry, and other accessories worn by jurors? Do you observe what they carry; lunch bags and such that jurors bring with them to court? Have you ever noticed the titles of the books and magazines that the jurors may bring with them for the day? These are icons of meaning, in many cases, as they represent things of importance to that juror.

When you are permitted to ask questions, do you inquire about the juror's favorite bumper stickers, books, and movies, all of which may provide clues about what motivates a juror, i.e., what values that juror holds? While time will rarely permit it, consider the power of asking jurors for their favorite childhood stories. You may be surprised to know that a juror's drives and needs are often conveyed through the characters and stories they hold dear. For example, what kind of background might a person have whose memorable childhood story is "The Ugly Duckling," or perhaps *The Secret Garden*? Through personal experiences in which these stories were cited by persons, there were many ties noted between that person's values and his or her memories of the story. Many a pain, gain, or memory is locked inside the childhood story that stands at the forefront of our memory. Learning juror metaphors can also help the lawyer shape the account and evidence accordingly, by

13 "Metaphors of Identity: Operating Metaphors & Iconic Change." (Genesis II, Longmont, Colo., 1991).

including some reference to the types of values incorporated in the opening and closing.

You may wish to work into your opening statement and closing argument certain anecdotes or analogies that involve metaphors of importance for the jurors. For example, if during voir dire you learned the jurors' favorite childhood stories or a meaningful bumper sticker (but be certain the bumper sticker was placed on the vehicle by the juror himself or herself and not by a relative with access to the family car), you may wish to work that into your opening statement or closing argument and then return to the elements of that information that tie to the reality you seek to create through your evidence.

Take, for instance, the juror who notes the story of the ugly duckling. In closing, and if appropriate, the lawyer can ascribe to the plaintiff in a personal-injury case the qualities and characters of an underdog who might now be rejected by other members of society. Could anything be more powerful for that particular juror, as well as others who will relate to the argument on a level that is other than conscious?

To develop this skill at a higher level, take some time outside the courtroom, perhaps at home or in the office, to ask people what type of animal, plant, song, book, article of clothing, color, place, instrument, activity, vehicle, sport, etc., they would be if they were such a thing at present. Then ask which of these metaphorical identifications they would *like* to be. Finally, ask them to describe the process through which their expected current identification would transfer them into the desired identification. The driving force that guides the transformation is a telling and powerful guide for that person.

For example, suppose your paralegal says he or she now

identifies with jazz music, but given the chance to be any kind of music, he or she would choose to be classical music. Asked how that transformation from jazz to classical would occur, imagine the following response: "The pumped-up and soulful jazz sounds would merge into a melodic pattern, filling out and expanding to include strings and other instruments, until they created a rich classical flavor." (If this example is a bit funky for you, it happens to be a real example from a person who practiced this exercise). What have you learned about the respondent's driving force? It suggests, possibly, that the person seeks options, fullness, and a mellowing course.

During deliberations, would this person not attempt to resolve the case in a similar pattern? People are creatures of habit, and we resort to familiar processes. Under stress, we are even less likely to seek new roads of creativity, so if they can identify their driving forces metaphorically, then they will do so in their deliberations as well.

If this all makes sense, then return to the childhood story for a moment. Now consider learning, if time permitted in voir dire, the following information about a juror's favorite childhood story:

- Describe the main characters of the story.
- What was the main character's purpose? Goal?
- What did you like about the story? What did it do for you?
- What did the story mean to you, say to you? What was its value?

Time permitting (and it rarely will), ask jurors to retell their favorite story, changing it, as they wish, to end as the jurors wish it would have ended. Let jurors feel free to add resources to characters, to add a sense of recognition for the characters. Don't be surprised if the qualities the jurors add to the main characters are not the same qualities the jurors wish they had in their own lives.

Does this provide information on the jurors' decision-making styles? Once again, consider using the gathered information during this voir dire exercise appropriately and meaningfully in closing argument. Incorporate the characteristics and resources the jurors would add to create a powerful reality. Give them what they seek and create a sense of comfort for them.

This is not a technique many lawyers will have time to exercise in voir dire. Truth is, you might be better advised to try this technique with a client as a means of getting to better know that person and how he or she views life. Even if you never use this technique at all, if you plug into the value, the purpose, the intent of this exercise, you are nevertheless likely to be more sensitive and in tune with other people just by being aware of the processes.

The power of life metaphors are best explained through the type of information each of you can relate to within the scope of your own life. In trial, you will gain greater insight into the jurors through the information you are able to gather when asking about favorite books, movies, or magazines. Look deeper into the answers and try to identify the values and attitudes that drive those people. You can expect these same values and attitudes to guide their in-court decision-making process as well.

PART V.

THE LAWYER'S DOMAIN

CONSTRUCTING REALITY AT TRIAL

Opening Statements
Examination
Closing Arguments

And Your Point Is?

Taking Control of the Case in the Opening Statement

L adies and gentlemen of the jury, during this opening statement you will hear the story of my client, Alexandra Brickton, who fell on some ice in the hallway of the Naldo Hotel. This is my opportunity to talk to you directly about what the evidence will show. Once the evidence is in, you will see that my client is entitled to a substantial amount of money."

With these words, attorney Richard Keith believes he has captured the jurors' attention. Probably nothing could be further from the truth.

The opening statement is supposed to be a road map for understanding. It takes on special importance because throughout the trial and into their deliberations the jury will remember what they are promised during the opening statement. The opening becomes a gauge for a reality used by the jury as it listens to the testimony and accounts being offered. If a lawyer fails to meet what he or she promises to produce, the jury will lose trust in that lawyer.[14]

Each lawyer should create and monitor a list of promises made by the opponent during his or her opening statement. In this way, both the jury and lawyer can hold the other side responsible for proving what it promises and not permit compelling but unsubstantiated rhetoric to stand unchallenged.

There are two components to relating the account at trial in an effective manner. The first is to tell the story in terms that jurors can comprehend, and the second is to help the jurors interpret the evidence in a manner desired by that lawyer. The lawyer needs to assist the jurors in making sense out of all that will be offered into evidence.

The pieces of the story need to be put together coherently by the jurors, a process that is guided by the lawyers. As you consider jurors listening to your opening statement, you need to consider how the other side might tell *your* version of events: factors that would change and switch from the other side's perspective. Be able to respond to those differences. Try determining what the other side's version of those events will be, as well.

How would you respond to what the other side says? What components of your own story would you change or switch to

---

14 Irving Younger. *The Advocate's Deskbook: The Essentials of Trying a Case.* (Clifton, NJ: Prentice Hall Law & Business, 1988).

meet what the other side could say? Monitor this information throughout the opening and throughout the trial. Perhaps most importantly, you will want to integrate the adversary's theme or story into your own. Address it directly and help the jury understand how your account meets the challenges of the other side's version of events, but also how it moves *beyond* the other side's story in a compelling fashion.

An opening statement needs to introduce and orient the jury to the case theme, establish rapport with the court and jury, maintain the jury's attention, and provide the jury with a recognizable and consistent accounting of events. An effective opening is persuasive yet simple.

For some reason, many a lawyer wastes the first moments of the opening statement. They get caught up in defining what an opening is, what purpose it serves, where the trial goes next, what role the lawyer will play, and so forth. With any luck, they finally begin to discuss the case several minutes into the presentation. Unfortunately, by that time the jury is long tuned out, albeit well educated as to the theoretical functions of an opening statement.

Another ineffective route is the lawyer who knows the case so well that she or he acts as if the jury also must be quite familiar with the facts. This is an extremely common difficulty, attorneys acting as if the jurors (and sometimes their clients, too) have the same history with the case. They do not! To compound the problem, the lawyer speaks as though he were delivering the opening statement to a room full of nuclear scientists, or more often, a room full of fellow lawyers.

These lawyers forget the basics and speak above the understanding of the jury. This mistake can cost them the jury's attention for good. Failing to give jury members a hook to grasp may push them to seek comfort from the other side's account of the case.

Why not make the opening a powerful presentation—one that captures the attention of jurors and relates a compelling, consistent, and complete accounting of events as well as the things that will be presented through the evidence? The reality is that jurors have a short attention span. (Don't we all?) They will listen intently for the first minute or two, but then, because they are human, they will find their minds wandering away. The best moments, which many lawyers use to define the process of an opening statement, have now been wasted.

Begin your opening statement with a powerful phrase, one that captures the tone and message of the continuity. Consider what trial consultant Richard Crawford calls "firing your silver bullets."

As you stand up to speak, you have more depth of juror attention than you will ever have again. You must immediately take your best shot, so fire your silver bullets.[15]

Begin by establishing the account by immersing the jury into it, not by announcing you are about to give an opening statement. For example, avoid beginning with "Ladies and gentlemen, this is a case about something you'll hear later, but first let me explain what an opening statement is and does for the first fifteen minutes of my time!"

Rather, consider the following examples:

In a personal injury case (plaintiff): "This case is about safety on the job, about a man who lost his arm while doing his job,

---

15 *The Persuasive Edge.* (New York: Wiley Publications, 1989), 110.

about a man who worked for the same company for twenty years, a man who can no longer do his job. But this case is much more, because we will show that this man, Owen Burr, did not need to lose his arm, that this man had his arm taken from him because he was asked to operate a piece of machinery unsafe for human use. When Owen was asked to operate this machine, he did not hesitate, because he had a good-faith trust in his company, a trust which made him believe he would not be sent to a job with equipment which would harm him."[16]

From a defense perspective in a personal injury case: "A little time, a little care, a little caution. That's all it would have taken to avoid the unfortunate accident that occurred in this case. A little time…to read the instructions and manual, a little care… in assembling the machine, a little caution…in turning on the power and working with the machine. But if you rush and you don't pay attention and you throw caution to the wind, then you end up in court pointing fingers at the company that did exercise time, care, and caution in the design, manufacture, and use of an admittedly dangerous machine."

Note how the opening statement provides a theme that can be returned to, time and again throughout the trial. "Once the appropriate theme is determined, counsel plants that theme in the minds of the jury in and through the opening statement. He or she then emphasizes it through questioning of witnesses, and pulls it through again in summation."[17]

One must be careful not to lose the art in the exercise of proper technique.

---

16   Ibid, p. 112.
17   Ronald J. Matlon. *Communication in the Legal Process.* (New York: Holt, Rinehart and Charles Inc., 1988), p. 180.

The Noise in My Head Is Deafening

Opening Statement: Getting Past the Barriers inside Jurors' Minds

There are potential barriers that can frustrate the transmission of the lawyer's message during the opening statement. Jurors' past experiences and existing attitudes, values, and beliefs will distort their reception and perception of the message. They serve as a filter through which the attorney's words must pass. It is not surprising that the psychological noise in jurors' heads can lead to interpretations of information that don't even occur to the lawyer.

For example, if a juror believes a witness is lying, then the witness's testimony will be discounted by that juror and determined to be incredible. Similarly, if the juror fails to understand the message because it has been related in a way that the particular juror can't follow, then little of the message's intended meaning will be assimilated. This psychological noise can also be triggered by juror disinterest, illness, inattention, anger not related to the trial, or mental argument with each concept offered by the lawyer in opening statement.

Noise may also occur in a more tangible way. Poor acoustics, a soft speaking voice that renders the message inaudible, or other physical distractions can present a barrier to the creation of communication among lawyers, witnesses, and jurors. Constant objections and sidebars trigger questions in jurors' minds; they want to know what they're missing and desire to make sense of information they don't even have or are not given.

Noise exists for the juror whose life views are challenged in voir dire by attorneys. If a lawyer contradicts the presumption a juror has about her world and the case at hand, in that juror's mind—either directly or by implication—a great deal of psychological noise is generated by that juror.

How can this be avoided? By asking the right questions in jury selection, questions that reveal the underlying attitudes and values of the jurors. That information must be integrated into the lawyer's opening statement, not ignored in favor of a statement drafted in final form before jury selection ever takes place.

In a practical sense, it means the lawyer must edit and rewrite the opening statement just before delivering it to ensure that the jurors who will hear and decide the case will relate to the lawyer. They hear back the very words and concepts they previously related in voir dire as important to them. If the lawyer gives an opening statement properly and with congruence, the jurors will gain significant respect for that lawyer.

Consider delivering the opening statement as you would when speaking to a friend. Rather than saying, "We submit, ladies and gentlemen," try this: "You know what happened here? This man walked into the bank and..." This is not to suggest a compromise of formality or importance. It is more a reflection of the need to establish rapport with each juror. The way to do so is to create commonality between lawyer and juror, and this is furthered through a knowing and approachable style.

To ensure reaching all jurors, prepare your opening statement as follows:[18]

1. Outline, but do not write out verbatim, the entire opening statement.
2. Pay close attention to the central points that must be communicated effectively to all jurors.
3. Draft each key point so that it can be delivered effectively; use auditory-based words, visual-based words, and feeling-based words accompanied by their associated gestures. This can be accomplished through the use of exhibits or models to which the parties have stipulated (or simply by referencing their upcoming presentation), and by incorporating components of logic with a sense of emotion (tied to your modeling of kinesthetic processing).

If you know where you will place a graphic during the course of the trial, indicate that spot with your hands, even if the exhibit is not yet placed in the indicated space. Never fear

18   From Lisnek and Oliver. *Courtroom Power: Communication Strategies for Trial Lawyers.* (PESI Law Publications, 2001).

holding up the "invisible" exhibit and attributing great potential to it when it finally appears. Be certain, however, that when it does, you are holding it in exactly the same fashion, standing exactly on the same spot, and referencing it with exactly the same terms with which you "previewed" it. In this way, you can use questions to establish the presence of things to be seen later and even things not to be seen.

For example, in one case where the lawyer wished to create the impression of a small, near claustrophobia-inducing room, he spread his arms wide to describe more reasonable rooms, but he crouched to create what it was like to step into the room involved. The jurors could relate and likely felt the sensation.

It may seem obvious, but it is essential that lawyers avoid the use of legalese in favor of common, user-friendly terms and phrases. Remember that you must be understood by the least educated juror. This applies even to the operative terms of the courtroom. If you must use a term of art, pause as you check the jurors' faces to monitor their comprehension. If they seem confused, then return to the term and offer a more palatable definition.

Effective opening statements do not require the lawyer (plaintiff lawyer, for example) to set out a request for an exact damage figure. In fact, as a rule, the plaintiff's lawyer is best advised to avoid stating a specific dollar amount to sink in and be established. The jury always requires justification, regardless of the amount requested.

The lawyer is advised, however, to indicate to the jury that a "significant amount" of damages will be sought and requested in the case. Jurors will likely come to expect a dollar figure by the time of closing argument that is even higher than the lawyer actually requests! I consulted in a personal injury case where the trial judge refused to allow the plaintiff's lawyer (my client) to reference or specify any money designated beyond "significant" in the voir dire. Frustrating for both lawyer and juror alike, it seems necessary that a lawyer be permitted to forecast the parameter of damages. "Significant" is millions to a lawyer, but may be thousands to a juror.

Integrate these ideas, and you create a framework for an opening statement that is both of appropriate content and elegance.

A Lie of Mythical Proportions

Concentrate on the Unstated in Opening Statements

It is an old myth that in 80% of all cases, jurors make their minds up after opening statements. Citing Kalven and Zeisel's *The American Jury*, many lawyers believe the towel need be tossed in with a poor opening statement. Guess what? Not true. Kalven and Zeisel never found such a conclusion to be true and, in fact, Zeisel confirmed for me in a conversation before his death that the mysteriously based conclusion had no basis in fact.

If you read *The American Jury*, you not only will not find the research conclusion noted above, you won't even find the words "opening statement" in the book. I asked Professor Zeisel from where he thought this mythical finding emerged. He had no idea. He was aware that he and Kalven were cited as sources for the finding, but could not explain where or why it had been created. In fact, prior to his death, he published an article addressing this point and saying that jurors did not make up their minds after opening statements.

I decided I needed to dig deeper into this inquiry. The conclusion itself made no sense to me and shouldn't to you, when you reflect on it. If jurors make up their minds in most cases after the opening statement, then why even have a trial? You might as well give the openings and then poll the jurors and call it a day. I don't know of a lawyer that would practice law in this way.

I worked with some colleagues years ago to address the question of when it is that jurors do make up their minds; and from the onset of the research, it was striking and clear that the research question was the wrong one. We aren't interested in when people make up their minds or come to an unmovable conclusion. At that point in time, the game is over. Moreover, it's not how people make decisions in the real world. For example, we don't wake up one day and decide to buy a new car and then go buy it. No, we go through a period of evaluation and analysis. On day one, we may wake up and realize that we need a new car, so begin to lean toward buying one; but simultaneously, or close enough to that point in time, we also realize that it may not be the best time economically to buy an expensive item. The next day, we do some research and realize that we can buy a *used* car at a much lower price, but we're also not sure if we want to deal with the potential problems of a used car. The point is, human beings do not just wake up and reach a conclusion; we begin to lean at a certain point in time and then we test, evaluate, and analyze and ultimately, through a process of leaning back and forth, we begin to commit to a final position. Ultimately, we make a decision.

In a jury setting, the process is no different. Jurors will begin to lean at some point; and we know that once people begin to lean, they will seek out evidence that supports their position. That much is human nature. In the research done to study this question, we found that most jurors began to lean during (or as a result of) the presentation of the cases in chief by both sides. Some jurors began to lean after the plaintiff presented its case; other jurors did not lean until the defense presented its responsive case in chief. Interestingly, the fewest number of mock jurors in the research reported that they first began to lean during the opening statements or closing arguments of the lawyers. Sorry to break the news, but according to the research, the fewest number of jurors were persuaded to the point of first leaning at all by what the lawyers said. Rather, jurors waited for the evidence, just as they are supposed to do.

In many ways, the research result was good news. Jurors listen to evidence, first begin to lean, and then may seek evidence that supports their leaning. That's okay, because strong contrary evidence can bring jurors back in the other direction. In any case, what we do know is that the ball game is not over after opening statements...in fact, it never was!

What do jurors listen to in opening statements? They listen closely in opening statements for the promises that are made by each lawyer and the completeness and consistency of the presented accounts. Most jurors defer to and follow the judge's lead at every stage of the trial. Many will focus their attention on the judge while they listen to testimony, opening statements, and closing arguments. Most will be profoundly affected by the judge's position, her robes, gavel, and the attendant flag and bailiff, to say nothing of the fact that she is usually perched much higher than anyone else in the room. These distinctions are not lost on jurors.

Because up to 93% of the impact of the messages passed in that courtroom is nonverbal, it is not surprising that the judge works to develop a high level of rapport among the jurors. The lawyer should consider adopting some of the judge's postures and general motions, while avoiding mimicry, both while delivering the opening and also while listening to the opposing side's opening. It is not uncommon for some of that juror-judge connection to pass to a lawyer who fits the same mold. One exception was a case in which I assisted in jury selection. The judge's no-nonsense demeanor was displayed for lawyer and jurors alike. This created a group of disgruntled jurors who looked to the lawyers for comfort, not the court. My personal opinion is that this was a poor strategy choice by the judge, if in fact it was conscious.

Everyone has indicators of agreement and denial (a nod, a shrug) that are consistent and evident in behavior. Because jury members respond poorly to perceived coercion or manipulation of their attitudes, you should present your points in your opening, without hammering the point home nonverbally. You might run the risk of being perceived by the jury as the nonverbal equivalent of a pushy salesperson who forces his position onto unwilling others.

It is much more elegant to present, at first, a generally neutral position. As you see juror agreement signals emerge indicating only their understanding of your point, then it is time to follow suit by responding in kind to their agreement, fed back to them as if it were yours. It is the nonverbal equivalent of such simple etiquette that no one would ever doubt its effectiveness at the verbal level. What you are doing is simply making an assertion about your case and then waiting for your listeners to agree that they got the message, instead of answering for them.

If you want to see for yourself the difference this simple courtesy can make for the subjective impressions of the receiver, get an associate and try this simple experiment.[19] First, assert several points as true and drive them home simultaneously by nodding, smiling, and so forth. Then make the same assertions, but this time hold still until the listener has the chance to react before you nod along with him or her. The difference in the level of sensations associated with each version can be striking.

Remember that you have the power to embed *meaning* in jurors' minds. One way to do this in an opening statement is through anchoring. Repetition of specific triggers at definitive times links an immediate responsive connection between the stimulus and response. In the courtroom, the lawyer can use her or his hands and body to place truth and untruth in different locations. For example, referring to the truth of what the jury will hear from that lawyer's witness can be emphasized by standing in a particular space or pointing to a specific place in space.

To the contrary, the veracity of the testimony to be presented by the other side can be brought into question by moving the body to another space or shifting the arms to a new location.

19 Lisnek and Oliver. *Courtroom Power: Communication Strategies for Trial Lawyers.* (PESI Law Publications, 2001).

The jury observes the placement of truth in one location and untruth in another.

The technique becomes more powerful as this movement and use of space is repeated throughout the course of the trial, in testimony, and again during closing arguments. Soon the jury will understand what is true and what is not true, merely by watching the movements of the lawyer as they repeat or trigger the anchor for the jury. It is wise to begin this "placement" of true and untrue anchors with indisputable truths and then move into those truths that might be less apparent.

Words and phrases can be introduced or reinforced from voir dire, as well. Terms such as "ripped off," "smashed," "crashed," or "responsibility and accountability" can be anchored and triggered throughout the opening and trial. These words, if they originate from a juror's mouth, are anchors. In truth, every word is an anchor for the speaker. You can integrate words and phrases the jurors use in voir dire to bring the meaning of the case, as you tell it, closer to home; i.e., within the reality of that juror. Also, spatial and gestural anchors can provide a powerful foundation for jurors to build on as your account unfolds along the road you've mapped out.

Metaphors can create a new and powerful reality in the courtroom by tying the lawyer's or party's message to the internal dialogue and driving forces of the jurors. In its simplest terms, the use of metaphor in opening (repeated in closing) permits jurors to find the reality of the case in their own life's experiences.[20] If you embellish this trend with those metaphors used or implied by jurors in selection, the impact can be multiplied significantly.

---

20 Charles Faulkner. "Metaphors of Identity: Operating Metaphors & Iconic Change," an audiotape series (Genesis II, Longmont, Colo., 1991).

Remember that, while we prefer the term "account" of the reality you wish to represent to the jurors, it is never smart to drift too far from the realization that all retellings of reality are skewed by the tainted memories of parties and witnesses and the bias of those people as well as the lawyer/advocate.

Continually monitor the telling of the story you are inviting the jurors to perceive, not from your point of view, but from the viewpoint of the people who must tell that story to themselves in a way that is most compelling for your client; and that would be the jurors. Done effectively, the jury is favorably postured in the opening statement for the testimony to come during direct and cross-examination. Their minds are set in a favorable direction. Let's take a closer look at the power of anchoring as it plays out in the courtroom.

"Anchors" Aweigh —
Helping Jurors Make
the Right Connections

Anchors as a Tool of Persuasion

First you don't see it, and then you do. While this may strike you as a bit strange and perhaps a reverse-order process, it is the fundamental explanation of the power of anchors in the courtroom. In addition to all of the documents, charts, graphs, and other evidence that will make their way into the jury's experience, lawyers have available to them another communicative technique that can be a powerful tool in grounding a concept in the minds of the jurors.

An anchor is the trigger that connects two things automatically in a person's mind. We are affected by hundreds of anchors all day long. For example, when the alarm goes off in the morning, we know instinctively that it is time to rise, get out of bed, and get ready for work. Most of us have a routine for dressing, everything in its place, and we get confused if anything is out of place. The anchors continue during the day, as we know to be hungry when the clock strikes noon, as we put the exact amount of cream in our coffee, as our assistants greet us in the same manner every morning, and so on and so on. You probably think of these as routines, and they are, but they are also the anchors that govern our behavioral actions and reactions.

Anchors are so ingrained in us that we don't even know they are there until one is absent. For example, we get flustered if we cannot find the car key, especially if it is always in the same place every day...until today. Have you ever awakened to the alarm, showered, and dressed and gone halfway out the door only to stop in your tracks when you finally realize that it is a holiday or a Sunday, and you are *not* heading into the office? Such is the power of an anchor. Of course in the law I am not sure this example reflects reality, as a day off is rare and far between.

Fortunately, anchors are easy to establish because they rely on repetition, instinct, and recognition. You likely remember learning of the famous experiments by Ivan Pavlov, who would ring a bell and then feed his dogs. Soon the dogs mentally tied the sound of the bell to the receipt of food, and they began to salivate upon hearing the bell, whether or not they were actually given any food. Human instinct is no different, except we are smarter and quicker to make the tie between anchor and the object or goal of that anchor.

How do we use this naturally occurring response effectively at trial? When a lawyer wishes the jury to make a connection between any two things, an anchor is a useful device. For example, suppose that you want the jury to get a sense that your expert has been more accurate and truthful than the other side's expert. In addition to the power of words and evidence, an anchor can be established to assist with this purpose.

For example, you might stand in one spot in front of the jury as you discuss what is clearly uncontroverted testimony of witnesses that has been presented. Then you would shift to another spot when it is time for you to discuss clearly contrary and incredible evidence. You then shift back to the first spot as you present additional uncontested information and back to the second spot for more questionable evidence. A repetition of this behavior three or four times establishes in the minds of the jurors where you have placed truth and where you have placed (or anchored) untruth.

Soon the jurors come to internalize where truth rests and where it does not. It is not long before you can step into the spot where truth has been anchored and notice how instantaneously the jurors react. Shortly it becomes unnecessary to mention which testimony is truthful and which is not; you merely need to stand in the representative spots. Be careful, however, as the jurors will have the anchor triggered simply by your stepping into that same space, whether or not you wish them to do so.

An audience member in one of my public jury psychology CLE seminars told me that during one trial, he took off his glasses as he sat at counsel's table and while conducting cross-examination. He did so, he told me, so he could see the witness, as he could not do so while wearing what were reading glasses. The jurors anchored his removal of the reading glasses to what they now perceived as untruthful testimony coming from the witness. The lawyer learned this after the trial when a juror reported to him, "Hey, we knew when those witnesses were lying during the direct examination conducted by your opponent." When the lawyer asked the jurors how they came to that conclusion, the jurors responded, "Because whenever you took your glasses off during the direct examination, we knew you recognized the lie!" The lawyer shared with me that there was no intended action; he removed his reading glasses simply to be able to better see the witness, because he could not do so with them on!

Through repetition of this behavior during his destructive cross-examinations, the lawyer unknowingly established an anchor, the influence and effect of which was felt as the jurors evaluated what they had heard on his opponent's direct exams. In this case, the anchor, if intentional, could be considered to be an unethical attempt to influence or disrupt the testimony. Unknown to the lawyer, it is simply an unrecognized influence.

Anchors also are a powerful tool to establish an atmosphere that cannot be created through pictures or diagrams. I once consulted in a case in which the lawyer needed to establish (as part of his case) the tight, almost claustrophobic atmosphere of a particular building. He did not know how to do this, because a review of photos of this and other similar buildings didn't serve to establish the necessary sense for the jurors. In my work with him on the use of anchors, he learned to describe the other buildings with very broad gestures, creating a sense of spaciousness. Then, when it was time to discuss the subject building, he closed in his body, brought his hands in and stood before the jury in a position that suggested he was experiencing a very tight space.

Through repetition of this movement in his ongoing description, it did not take very long at all until the jurors strongly sensed the smallness of the environment he was suggesting. This was an important element in the case, and every juror came to understand the power of this fact. It is important to note that many lawyers would also have described the space through the use of an appropriate metaphor or analogy; however, it was important that this lawyer get the jury to experience kinesthetically, through feeling, the specifics of this environment. By triggering the desired feelings, the lawyer reached well beyond having the jurors relate; he led them to experience something he needed them to feel. Now that's power!

Clearly all lawyers use gestures and move about the courtroom all the time, albeit within the bounds of propriety. What I am suggesting is that we unknowingly establish anchors throughout the trial. The issue is whether they will be handled knowingly and controlled (such as the compassion a criminal defense lawyer exhibits to his or her client while sitting at counsel's table), or unintended, yet influential nevertheless, though they occur out of our consciousness. The master trial lawyer is always in tune with the experiences of the jury. The acknowledgment and use of anchors at trial adds an important level to that control.

Isn't It True?

Unnerving the Witness during Direct and Cross

Undergoing direct or cross-examination can be unnerving for any layperson. Witnesses can be greatly comforted once they learn that the myriad questions they are asked boil down to three central areas: their background, the incident in question, and the injuries or damages incurred in the matter at hand.

The background of the witness refers to the relevant education, employment, or other factors from the witness's past that may reflect on his or her credibility. The incident in question involves what that witness knows, how he or she knows it, and any limitations on the knowledge. Finally, the consequences of the incident form the basis of damages claimed, so whatever the witness knows on that subject may be the subject of inquiry. Many witnesses find comfort in knowing that there is no question that can fall outside these three categories; that's nice news for a witness who previously feared a process that would be overwhelming.

Witnesses also need to understand the types of questions that may be asked of them. Reading the definition of an open, closed, or leading question is easy enough, but lawyers should not assume that such an explanation carries any deep meaning for the witness. There is enough pressure on witnesses in being in a strange environment of the courtroom and trial that the lawyer can assume witnesses are likely to forget whatever tricks of the trade are taught to them anyway.

The answer lies in providing the differences in question types through analogies. For example, comparing question types to the experience of walking down a hallway with a series of doors leading to various rooms can work nicely. Ask a witness, "Would you describe a room you have never been in? If not, pass that door and continue down the hallway. Would you, as you describe a room with which you *are* familiar, offer and volunteer the location of your secret hiding places and the value of your possessions? If not, then exert the same type of control during testimony."

To eliminate monotony and boredom during direct examination, lawyers should employ a variety of questioning techniques that reflect the type of information desired and the temperaments of the witness and the jury.[21] The form and wording of

---

21 James W. McElhaney, "McElhaney's Trial Notebook," (American Bar Association, 2nd ed., 1987).

questions will clearly dictate meaning. For example, consider the difference between asking, "How near to the vehicle were you?" and, "How far from the vehicle were you?" Each will produce a different response. Specifically, asking "How near?" will tend to produce a shorter distance.

The words lawyers use during both direct examination and cross-examination have more power than I can ever relate here. Many words are emotionally charged; others trigger no emotional responses or effect. Lawyers need to be masters of language who have a sense of elegance in structuring their questions, statements, and arguments. They need to ask questions in a way that doesn't inadvertently offend the values and attitudes of jurors. Remember, life filters are powerful and accompany us everywhere we go. They do not step out and leave a juror during deliberation. If a juror is skeptical of police evidence-collection procedures, then a defendant in a criminal case begins on uneven footing in his or her favor for that juror.

Moreover, people add and delete details to descriptions of their experiences, which taints the retelling and interpretations of experiences. Through questioning, the lawyer can focus attention on how witnesses or a party may have deleted, distorted, generalized, or limited the retelling of experiences. After all, the questions we ask determine the quality of the information retrieved. In addition, the manner in which a question is constructed may even lead the witness to re-evaluate his own thinking before answering under oath in court. This helps to explain the behavior of witnesses who testify to a truth no one has ever heard before!

Because meaning lies within the person, not in words, lawyers must seek memories and interpretations from the witness from that starting point, which is the form of events as they exist in the person's mind. For example, to suggest, "Why didn't you request a copy?" assumes that the respondent believes he should have made such a request. Or a witness may react to an emotionally charged word like "problem." Try replacing the word with "concern" or "issue," and watch the listener become more comfortable—if comfort is your aim. In preparing a witness for cross, for instance, it would probably not help to indicate where you expected him to have a "problem."

The word "but" negates whatever proceeds it, so replacing it with the word "and" will also produce a more positive interaction. Prefacing questions of your own witness with the word "but" has its dangers. If the witness has obscured part of the account you wished to emphasize and you interject with "But," the jury frequently takes this as if you were cross-examining your own witness.[22] A lawyer seeking additional information is better advised to ask "What else?" which presupposes the existence of something else, rather than the phrase "Anything else?" which does not. The latter phrase closes an open line of inquiry, regardless of how much more information that witness may have had to reveal.

Many lawyers draft their questions believing they are seeking particular information. If this were so, why would we not write down the answers, rather than the questions? The truth is, we fear *not* writing down the questions.[23] The secret to an effective direct examination is not to focus on the particular questions

---

22 Lisnek and Oliver. *Courtroom Power: Communication Strategies for Trial Lawyers.* (PESI Law Publications, 2001).
23 Herbert J. Stern. *Trying Cases to Win: Direct Examination..* (New York: John Wiley and Sons, 1992), 14.

you are going to use. Rather, think of the words you wish to hear from this witness, and in the witness's own words. In this way, the words of the most appropriate question will be most likely to emerge in your mind.

This is not to suggest that an outline should not be used, because it can be quite helpful. An outline will help both the lawyer and the witness uncover any holes or weaknesses in the testimony.[24] And remember to integrate the words and phrases that appear to have meaning for the jurors. Ask questions as the jurors would themselves ask them.

Ultimately, the lawyer's goal is to bring out the testimony on direct examination and confirm through cross-examination the information that supports the continuity being established. Since people, as a rule, resist attempts by others to modify their position or beliefs, the lawyer needs special tools to assist in placing a wedge between what a witness experiences as reality and the facts that a lawyer in the role of advocate seeks to develop with that witness on the stand.

---

24 Ronald Matlon. *Communication in the Legal Process.* (New York: Holt, Rinehart & Charles Inc., 1988), 216.

Sleight of Mouth: Breaking Connections

A Speaker's True Meaning Is Often Hidden

Attorney Denny Crane found that whenever he assumed what his client Alan Shore was trying to say, he was usually wrong. Even when negotiating a settlement with fellow lawyer Shirley Schmitt, he found that he needed a new strategy to really understand what others were actually saying to him.

Clearly the perspective of the receiver is the key to effective communication. Because each person's reality is grounded in his or her personal experiences and filtered through that person's unique biases, the subjective experience will dominate over any objective evidence to the contrary. We need to learn, linguistically, to open windows to the subjective perspectives of others.

At the most general level, it is vitally important to avoid the habit of translation. Don't assume that what a word or phrase means to us is what it means to anyone else; it likely does not mean the same thing. It is always better to ask the other person for the meaning and avoid making a presumption of the meaning.

Questions like "How do you see that?" or "How did you come to say that?" or "How would you know that?" clarify and add meaning. Most people do not object to this scrutiny: They appreciate the effort to be understood—and understood accurately—and the effort of their lawyer to make their case stronger.

Many people try to say what they mean, but almost by definition confusion can result. There are several specific strategies you can use to gain a better understanding of another person's speech and meaning. These techniques include the following:

Universal Quantifiers

Universal quantifiers are words that the user applies to all cases and situations, without exception. These include words like "all," "every," "always," "none," and "never." These words can be clarified by questions that point out exceptions to the assumed rule. Thus the statement, "No one would view the situation in a particular way," should be followed up by, "Never?" or, "Is there ever a time when a different view could exist?"

Modal Operators of Necessity

Modal operators of necessity are words suggesting an absence of choice. Words and phrases such as "have to," "must," "can't," "should," "it's necessary," or "impossible" can be modified by inviting the speaker beyond the limits of that phrasing. For example, "What stopped you, so far?" The question permits the speaker to review his or her intent and reconsider the possibilities that exist but that were not previously perceived.

Unspecified Nouns

If someone uses nouns unspecified as to people, places, or things, such as "those things," or "these people," the litigator can follow up with questions that seek specifics, including the standard "Who?" "What?" "Which?" and "How?" Thus, for the statement "Those people make things more complicated," the follow-up is, "Who are these people? What things specifically? How are they complicated?" It is important to remember that the specifics you will receive will not necessarily reflect the reality you expect, but it will guide you in the direction to take the conversation with your client, another attorney, or whoever is speaking.

Nominalizations

Nominalizations are finite labels transformed from an active process into things which in reality are not things. Nouns describe things that can (metaphorically) be put into a wheelbarrow; nominalizations cannot be reduced to that level. "Chairs," "books," and "trees" are all nouns; "frustration," "happiness," and "relationships," when put into a wheelbarrow through their use as nouns, become nominalizations. Nominalizations reduce perceived choice or power. Nominalizations can be translated back into a process through the lawyer's questions; thus the nominalization "frustration" could be followed by the inquiry, "How is that frustrating for you?" or "What's that like, specifically?" Happiness might be followed by, "What's happy for you?"

To instantly convert from label to behavior, add the word "acting," "acted," or "reaction" to nominalizations that identify emotional or mental processes for the speaker. For example, "He's mad" could be converted to "He's really acting mad."

Cause-Effect Implications

Cause-effect implications happen when a person ties some experience to another as a causal relationship. These phrasings address an implied "Why?" concerning the attitudes, positions, and actions of the speaker. The effective lawyer keeps in mind that there may be other explanations for the seeming effect. For example, if someone says, "You annoy me," implying that you are the only cause of her acting annoyed, the lawyer might discover other reactions (satisfied, curious, etc.) the speaker has had and open up new options through this redefinition: "That's not annoyance, that's embarrassment!" The lawyer also might challenge the front end of the equation—"Is it me as a person you react to that way? Was it my words? Was it something else entirely, or a combination of things?"—all of which may break up the fixed associations.

Mind Reading

Mind reading is the assumption by many that they can somehow know what others are thinking or feeling. An example of mind reading would be: "He never thinks about that," or, "She wouldn't want to proceed on that point." The follow-up would be, "How do you know?" A common example is one who says, "I know what is best for him." The inquiry "How do you know?" brings the mind reading into question. Mind reading needs to be challenged if you want to determine if the other party actually holds a particular view or has firsthand knowledge. It can be reflected back in your own speech to illustrate an understanding of what the other person has been trying to say.

Lost Performatives

Many people speak in generalizations. These are called lost performatives and include statements such as "It is wrong to…" or "That's the best thing." The follow-up to a lost performative would be "For whom?" thus asking, "Wrong for whom?" "Right for whom?" or "Good for whom?"

Lawyers and clients alike will fall into some semantic traps. Our job is to work through ambiguities in search of clarity. Linguistic structure becomes the best tool to partly uncover subjective meanings in people's speech. Once these windows into the subjective reality of clients, lawyers, judges, and jurors are opened, the diligent litigator has begun to develop a real edge in the appreciation and utilization of human communication in practice.[25]

---

25 This article is based on Paul M. Lisnek and Eric Oliver. *Courtroom Power: Communication Strategies for Trial Lawyers.* (PESI LAW Publications, 2001).

We'll Just See about That...

Direct Examination Creates Reality, Cross Tests It

Direct and cross-examination develop both the theme and story that is established before trial and also introduced during both voir dire and opening statements. Direct examination is the time for establishing the specific components of the story; cross-examination is the test of that reality conducted by the adversarial party who has an *alternative* reality to establish for the judge or jury. If the other side can bring into question the reality you seek to create, then the jury is left with too much of an option in deciding what happened. The importance of ensuring a properly and thoroughly prepared witness is essential, as is complete preparation by the lawyers.

Direct examination has several purposes, which include presenting a clear and credible version of that portion of the continuous account each witness is on the stand to testify about. In addition, direct examination should be memorable, so to be perceived as significant by the jury.[26] For the opponent, direct examination means a search for contradiction; we must work to anticipate which area will be picked up from the direct examination for focus during cross-examination. Perhaps for this reason alone, it is important that each witness a lawyer prepares to testify be subjected to rigorous rehearsal of cross-examination. This experience permits the witness an opportunity to understand firsthand what it means to face scrutiny of one's account or position.

Lawyer preparation for both direct and cross-examinations, at least by the time of trial, is usually not a concern in terms of document review and legal research; few lawyers would ever walk into a trial with less than complete control over the facts and the controlling law. The success of a case often lies in the effectiveness of witnesses on the stand. It is essential to work with key witnesses until they know their testimony and understand its importance.

An attorney who would never dream of walking into court shaky on any point of fact or law about her case is remarkably the same lawyer who walks into that same courtroom and, in that same case, is shaky about the expected performance of one or more of the witnesses. The simple truth is that lawyers do not take the

26 Herbert J. Stern. *Trying Cases to Win: Direct Examination.* (New York: John Wiley and Sons, 1992), 11.

time necessary to prepare their clients and witnesses to testify. Put them on videotape (properly identified on the tape as attorney-client privilege or work-product protected) and let them see how effective they are or are not. Witnesses improve by experiencing the process. The theoretical becomes a practical reality when they actually undergo the expected cross-examination, learning to control their disclosures by experiencing what it means to volunteer information. Permit the witnesses to understand how their testimony fits within the overall case; they need to know the piece of the overall puzzle they provide. The commitment to tell the truth is not often enough to overcome the discomfort and uncertainties that occur on the witness stand; the latter can be read by jurors and therefore challenge credibility. This can lose the case of the lawyer.

Consider the result of inadequate witness preparation coupled with a lawyer who holds little faith in the skill of the witness to testify effectively. Neither witness nor lawyer will have a place to hide in that courtroom!

The lack of faith or belief can both kill a case and be broadcast to the jury or judge with a subtle, but extremely telling shift in the lawyer's voice tone, volume, or rate of speech; posture, tip of the head, or animation in his gestures all while introducing a witness in whom he holds little faith. There is a range of strengths and weaknesses for every witness, some at the high end, some not. It will be the attorney who feels most certain in the evaluation of these factors.

The point is, to quote the famous playwright Eugene Ionesco, "It is not the answer that enlightens, but the question." Often lawyers put the blame on the witness who experiences difficulty on the stand, whether on either direct or cross-examination. After introducing your witnesses to the expectations or requirements of their role, to the limits on the questioning they can expect, and to the nature of cross-examination, you would do well to shift your attention to the manner in which the testimony is most effectively presented to the jurors. Some language may be natural for the witness and anticipated by the jury. Television lawyer characters are well liked for a reason, because television lawyers are brief, to the point, and speak in dramatic, engaging language. Why do we lose these qualities once we step into the courtroom? Not only is the television lawyer often a model to be mirrored, but it's the only contact with the process that many members of the public will have before actually serving in a case. For better or worse, it's the way it is.

Give any witnesses you perceive to be uncomfortable ample time to express that feeling fully before rushing in to reassure them. Most witnesses can be assisted to improve in their testimony. Your witnesses, especially experts, will be best equipped to weave their testimony and answers on cross-examination into the continuity of your account if they have the complete story available to them. Point out the trial road map to your client or witnesses, and show them what visual exhibits, if any, their testimony will support and those that support their testimony. Emphasize the key phrases they will use in the testimony and the phrases their testimony will support. Although the actual chronology of their testimony may not match what you have described to them, having the trial road map in their heads can be critical to help them avoid hesitation, the appearance of confusion, or in the case of an expert, commentary that—although legally relevant or scientifically accurate—dilutes or distracts from the focus you want to maintain. To this end, particularly for those lawyers who have colleagues prepare the bulk of their witnesses for trial, having sketches or small mock-ups of demonstrative evidence to be presented at trial (if the case reaches that stage) can be extraordinarily useful for everyone to envision the map of the case.

It is true enough that the best-prepared witnesses can handle themselves even with the very best cross-examining lawyer. Accomplished witnesses learn the game: They come to understand that they can't really win the battle of cross-examination; they merely need to withstand the siege. They are prepared to hold their own ground and not be led into contradiction, confusion, or areas in which they lack knowledge.

Once witnesses come to understand cross-examination as little more than a speech given by the opposing attorney, the process is quickly deflated to a more comfortable, less troubling experience.[27] Cross-examination might be seen as an interview in which the lawyer seeks to extract a confirmation of certain points. Once the main points for cross-examination are uncovered, questions should be asked so that they sound like statements, rather than questions. For example, "You did read the contract before signing it, didn't you?" Questions asked like statements turn the question into a commentary. The use of this approach renders the witness somewhat irrelevant.

A lawyer can assist the witness on direct examination by paying attention to how that person prefers to process information; that is, through seeing, hearing, or feeling. The lawyer should draft questions that will permit each witness to process

27 Richard Crawford. *The Persuasive Edge.* (New York: Wiley Press, 1989), 152.

information in the way most comfortable for that person. The converse, of course, is true for creating discomfort, and even confusion, in a witness on cross-examination.[28]

For example, constructing questions that ask a witness who is predominantly visual to "describe, show us, or clarify" will create greater comfort in that witness than auditory requests such as "tell us" or "talk about." The converse is also true; auditory-based requests to a visual person can instill discomfort until that witness effectively translates the request to visual terms. Communication is not about us; it's about the receiver of communication. We have a responsibility to step into the world of the witness and balance in the jury's reality as well. No one said being a master trial lawyer would be easy.

One way a lawyer can keep the witness on track while still permitting the emphasis of favorable and important information is through the use of loop-back questions. This question form includes the answer given in the prior question. The question form usually avoids an objection to repeating the witness's answer. For example, "Now, you've said that the goods showed up on Thursday. On that date, did you then...?"[29] While looping back in this fashion, the attorney recasts the previous statement in her demeanor to match the sensory preferences of the judge, the jury, or the actual experience being described (auditory for a telephone conversation, visual for an eyewitness account, kinesthetic for commentary on pain and suffering). Once reaching the point of the succeeding inquiry, the attorney

---

28   Lisnek and Oliver. *Courtroom Power: Communication Strategies for the Trial Lawyer.* (PESI Law Publications, 2001).

29   Ronald Matlon. *Communication in the Legal Process.* (New York: Holt, Rinehart & Charles Inc., 1988), 226.

would then shift back to the witness's preferred mode for the core of the question.

Also consider the tempo and pace of the examination. While direct examination will vary with the style and comfort of the witness, the lawyer on cross-examination is more likely to create a rhythm. The tempo of the cross-examination would quicken, with each question being asked more rapidly than the preceding one.[30]

In many ways, conducting a witness examination is like a dance. The lawyer leads, the witness follows, and the case theme and moment determine the tempo and rhythm. The unskilled dancer sticks out on the dance floor, and the sad part is that while the onlookers laugh at the absence of rhythm or style, the dancer proceeds under the illusion of being Fred Astaire or a contestant on *Dancing with the Stars*! The courtroom is no different. The answer rests in proper, ongoing preparation of key witnesses. Practice the dance and get the rhythm down. At worst, the examination appears as a by-the-numbers interaction but does what it needs to do; at best, the examination proceeds with the admirable grace of a ballet, and in the case of cross-examination, it moves with the spicy admissions of a well-performed tango!

---

30   Lawrence J. Smith and Loretta A. Malandro. *Courtroom Communication Strategies.* (New York: Kluwar Law Book Publishers, 1985), 741.

Cross My Heart...

Mastering the Art of Cross-Examination

Having just completed the cross-examination of a witness, attorney Tom Mulroy takes a deep breath and says, "Ah, that wasn't so bad. Ya know, this cross-examination stuff isn't as tough as everybody says."

Partner Anne Brody puts her arm around Mulroy and says, "You're a bit naïve, my friend. You see, the technical part of cross-examination is not so difficult, but just doing what the books tell you isn't good enough. What did you really accomplish, except for getting the witness to confirm everything he said on direct? In addition to the technical aspect of cross-examination, you also need a certain degree of innate talent."

Cross-examination is not rehearsed, of course, so it becomes an exercise of courtroom improvisation.[31] For example, you need to consider whether the cross-examination should be an exercise in construction or destruction. When it needs to accomplish both, then you better conduct a constructive examination first and follow it with a destructive examination. To reverse the order would bring the witness's credibility into question and confuse the jury. After all, how do you go from attacking the credibility of the witness to using that same person as a credible source to confirm other points?

Consider the following example: "Dr. Mycroft, the truth is you have never written anything on the subject of this surgery, have you? In fact, you have no special training or certification in this area of medicine, do you?" Once the doctor agrees with these questions, the lawyer has significant difficulty turning the examination around to confirm some central point, one that only someone with expertise would address. The smarter path is to confirm whatever points are necessary and then, once confirmed, illustrate through questioning that the witness's credibility extends no further.

Certainly, the teachings of the late and great law professor Irving Younger and his "Ten Commandments of Cross-Examination" are worth repeating and keeping in mind as you prepare to cross-examine a witness. His commandments were and remain as simple as their message:

---

31   Roberto Aron, Julius Faust and Richard Klein. *Trial Communication Skills.* (New York: Shepard's McGraw-Hill, 1986), 261.

1. Keep the examination brief. Play the odds. There are so few effective cross-examiners, most lawyers best serve their efforts by bringing whatever they are doing to a swift close.

2. Use plain English. The jury will understand, and the odds improve that they will remain with you rather than doze off listening to technical or confusing language.

3. Use only leading questions. Once you open the door, an effective witness will take over the interaction.

4. Prepare to decrease the chance of being in a position of having to ask a question to which the answer is anything less than certain. This rule suggests a question should not be asked on cross-examination when the lawyer will not be able to refute confidently an undesired answer.[32]

5. Subordinate fears over what the next question will be by listening carefully to the witness's answers. In them often lies the direction for the next question and examination.

6. Avoid arguing with any witness. In the eyes of the jury, the lawyer will lose the battle and be seen as being unfair to the witness.

7. Do not use cross to repeat the direct. This is the sure sign of a poor cross-examiner.

8. Don't open the door to witness explanation. Once the witness takes the floor, it is nearly impossible for the lawyer to gain it back.

9. Don't ask the one-question-too-many. Get what you need and stop. It's that simple.

---

32 Paul Bergman. *Trial Advocacy in a Nutshell.* (St. Paul, MN: West Publishing Co., 1979), 183–186.

10. Keep your ultimate point for closing argument. In fact, recognize that the information gathered on cross becomes the food for closing argument.[33]

One more rule for cross-examination should be of value: End the examination as if you were able to elicit whatever information you wanted from the witness, no matter what actually happened.[34] Even when the testimony that gets elicited on cross-examination proves to be devastating to your case, respond as if you had wanted exactly that response. Hearing a hurtful answer, imagine the jury's reaction as they hear you exclaim, "Exactly! Thank you!" At a minimum, you will have deflected the damage and left jurors feeling as though that testimony was actually helpful to you.

Keith Evans suggests in his book *Common Sense Rules of Trial Advocacy* that when a bombshell falls unexpectedly in cross, the attorney should pause and dispassionately take note, as if it were expected from the witness's testimony. This enables the attorney to regroup, while implying to the jury that the testimony meant little and did no damage. This makes sense, because the alternative would be to blunder further into quicksand or to stand, with a gaping open mouth, in front of the witness. Even for those few litigators who steadfastly discount the power of a damaging piece of testimony on jurors, such negative body language would be considered poor form.

If the witness is clearly the star on direct examination, the lawyer is most certainly the star during cross-examination. On

---

33   Irving Younger. "The Art of Cross Examination." (American Bar Association, 1976), 21–31.

34   Noelle C. Nelson. *A Winning Case.* (Upper Saddle River, NJ: Prentice Hall, 1991), 262.

direct, lawyers carefully construct their questions to permit witnesses to speak with confidence and clarity. On cross-examination, the witness must merely hold his or her ground with whatever techniques the lawyer uses.

A lawyer who knows what to do on cross-examination will present what, in effect, plays as a speech. Merely punctuated by the simplistic short answers of the witness, the lawyer guides the testimony on cross-examination and should maintain control over the facts being put forth through questions. Once an open-ended question is asked, or an explanation is sought, the lawyer will watch as control shifts to the witness. If the witness is well prepared, he or she can seize the open-ended question to wrestle power from the ineffective lawyer.

On cross-examination, the lawyer is well advised never to ask a question to which the answer is unknown; however, you can never truly know what answer you will get from the witness. With a bit of reflection, it becomes clear that the lawyer may know what responses *should* be given, *must* be given, and just *have to be* given according to the evidence and testimony, and then the witness comes up with some answer out of left field that throws the examiner off completely. Should this occur, just make that knowing nod, as if the answer is *exactly* what you anticipated.

The best advice on cross-examination is to keep an open and flexible mind. Feel for and go with the rhythm of the witness—sense, guide, and control. Cross-examination is not as difficult as it is universally thought to be, but it is a far more difficult skill to perform with excellence and purpose than one can imagine.

That is why the *skill* of a lawyer may better be described as an art form.

Expert-tease

Expertly Turning the Tables on Experts

Dr. Beattner is a well-known orthopedist often called to testify in cases involving serious injury. As an expert witness, he is confident and controlled on the stand. Many lawyers are intimidated by his grasp of his field and fine execution of his testimony.

Attorney Melanie Grabavoy felt a bit jittery before beginning her cross-examination of the fine doctor. After all, this was one credible witness. Once Grabavoy reviewed her notes, she realized that all of Beattner's credentials did not serve to undermine her strategy. The plaintiff's injuries were severe but caused by something other than the events alleged. After distinguishing her case on its facts, Grabavoy was in much stronger control, and the cross-examination proceeded to her great satisfaction.

It's common to use an expert to clarify and interpret the significance of certain facts, all of which are encased in the vast experience and knowledge that expert has on a specific facet of the case. It is upon the strength of their qualifications that experts render their opinions. Because many experts make their living through testifying, the need for lawyer preparation prior to taking deposition or trial testimony is heightened. Even so, an expert's background can be a two-edged sword. For example, the expert engineer who works in an ivory tower may be attacked for spending too little time in the field. On the other hand, the engineer who labors in the field but lacks an academic post of which to boast may be seen as a hired gun without the crème-de-la-crème sheen of a prominent professor. A balance between academia and the field is most desirable, but every expert must sell his or her credentials to the jury. In sum, the field person ties credibility to extensive data and the tests conducted over the years; the academic highlights reputation and the fact that those in the field rely on what that expert has written and opined.

To enhance your sense of control over experts (and have a chuckle), consider the very word "expert." A friend of mine gave me real insight when he told me to break that word into syllables. Consider this definition: an "ex" is a "has-been"; and a "spert" is a drip under pressure! Keep in mind that experts, by definition, know more about their subject matter area than nearly all the lawyers who will question them. This is often the source of expert-imposed intimidation on lawyers, yet also remember that no one knows the facts of the case at hand better than does the lawyer. In fact, while an expert's work on a case rarely encompasses all that the expert knows, the application of that expertise concentrates on a smaller, more manageable subsection of knowledge. If this were not so, what purpose beyond boggling the jurors' minds would expert testimony serve? The most effective expert will learn to put aside the vast array of knowledge in favor of focusing on the key points of theory needed to educate the jury.

We can confuse ego with resistance when challenging an expert on the stand. When you think about it, what experts would admit to being wrong in their analysis as they testify? And why should they? The odds are that they know more about their topic than anyone on the jury, and they certainly do know more than any party or lawyer. Their best approach is to hang their hat on their own expertise. No matter what the inquiry, experts will find a way to control their testimony and will hold on strong to their theories.

When you think about it, don't most experts you know use a particular theory, rely on certain kinds of facts, and always crunch the numbers the same way in case after case? Most experts don't get to where they are in their careers without a strong theory or formula to implement, no matter what the case. It is unlikely, nor is it often necessary, that any lawyer will routinely challenge an expert's credentials unless there is some obvious reason to do so.

During direct examination, your experts know what you want them to accomplish, the phrases you want reinforced, and the role their testimony must serve in the overall road map you seek to craft for the jury in the case at hand. It is imperative that you know the limitations and weaknesses of your own expert, as well. Be sure you get those points of weakness out into the open for the jury before the cross examiner does it for you.

Prosecutors in the legendary O. J. Simpson murder trial learned the hard way. After the torturous experience of criminalist Dennis Fung under cross-examination by defense DNA expert Barry Scheck, the prosecution put on witnesses to address the various weaknesses Scheck was attacking. Why give the other side a shining moment when you can undermine the effect of cross-examination as being "been there, done that" in effect and thereby have jurors think of the weak points as old news?

How does one effectively deal with the opposing side's expert witness? The answer to controlling an expert witness usually lies not in attacking the expert's formula or theory but rather in focusing on the specific facts of the case or the methodology employed by the opposing expert. Special attention should be placed on the facts the expert relies on.

For example, I worked as a trial consultant in a case in which the plaintiff who had alleged a faulty home inspection retained an expert engineer, but the defendant's expert was not an engineer. The defendant contended the case was about home inspections and not engineering, and therefore argued the fact that the plaintiff's expert as an engineer was irrelevant in the case at hand.

The judge eventually barred the defense expert from testifying (as a matter of law), and the defendant proceeded to trial without an expert—and with less than perfect success. Contrary to what the plaintiff's attorneys believed, their expert never needed to be compelling in his credentials for a jury, but just for the judge. Once the judge accepted the engineer as the relevant expert for the plaintiff, the inspector working for the defense was automatically challenged on the basis of his credentials, engineering now being the accepted standard for the facts of this case.

By sticking to the facts of the case, the lawyer recognizes that every expert's testimony is, in fact, based on a certain set of facts processed in a particular way. All you need to do is replace the case facts relied on by the opposing expert in his or her equation with facts you provide, and watch the expert struggle to dodge their consideration. Where do you find the facts that will challenge the conclusion and possibly unnerve the expert? The best source for uncovering contradictory facts is your own expert. After all, your expert will likewise rely on a particular set of facts (that may get challenged by the other side, of course). Similarly, test the expert's method by illustrating the existence of alternate and equally applicable methods that would produce a contrary result. Again, your own expert can assist in identifying the alternative roads that best challenge the other side's expert.

Challenging the cause-effect relationship one side's expert puts forth based on specific facts will help the jury distinguish and separate expert credentials from relevant case facts. If sufficient questions are raised early on in the case, the jury can see through an expert's strategy, separating credentials from facts by the time that expert takes the stand, typically later in the case in chief.

The result is that the jury considers the opposition's experts with a healthy degree of skepticism. The proof will be in the experts' ability and willingness to handle alternative facts in their own theories or to apply alternative methods than the ones upon which they rely. Once you understand this approach, you can relax and work to keep experts on their toes—without being intimidated yourself.

Taking the
Last Word...

Closing Argument: Confirming Reality

Closing argument is often thought to be a moment of high drama. It is the moment that many lawyers wait for, to solidify their case. It is what jurors enjoy most as they partake in the many legal dramas that television has to offer. For the trial, closing argument is a time to confirm the truth of the evidence as it has come in. It is the time that the lawyers put it all together in what they hope are the powerful and persuasive moments of closing.

If the previous components of the case (essentially the parties' cases in chief) have not played out as intended or needed, however, then the closing argument will be too late to reach or appeal to the jury; thus, while many lawyers write the closing argument early in their trial preparation (because you have to know where you want to end up if you are to figure out where you need to go), the power of the closing argument rests strongly with the manner in which the evidence comes in through the course of the trial. Were the witnesses perceived to be as credible as you had hoped? Did the substance of what was offered through these witnesses weigh with impact on the jury, or did the jurors not find the case presented by the lawyers to be compelling, complete, or otherwise persuasive? Essentially, the closing argument is the culmination of a trial that should have been in the planning since the case first came in the office. Lawyers would be well advised to begin writing the closing after the case first comes in the office and discovery commences. Working up a case is not only about discovering information and details it's about testing and confirming facts. After all, why not ensure that depositions and other discovery are conducted so as to strengthen the case? The lawyer should not be left to explain away the details in the case during the trial that would have better have been shaped much earlier in the case and not at its pinnacle!

The meaning of evidence is perceived by the jurors, but is *shaped* by the lawyers. Lawyers need to understand how evidence may be perceived and given meaning by jurors as the lawyer shapes the closing arguments around these perceptions. It may be surprising to realize that the structure of a closing argument will emerge from the information, admissions, and confirmations gained through cross-examination. If you think about it, jurors expect and anticipate that direct examinations will merely confirm the story or continuity the lawyer seeks to present (and its failures to do so will weigh heavily on the jurors' evaluations). The real impact power lies in what is gained through the cross-examination of adversary witnesses and parties. Admissions gathered from adversarial witnesses will weigh strongly in the jurors' minds and perhaps more strongly than any expected testimony. The admissions and challenges accomplished in cross-examination become the powerful elements of the closing argument, because this is information not offered in one's own self-service, as your own friendly witnesses' direct examination. It is powerful because it is culled from people adversarial to your position and grounded in testimony not designed to assist your case.

In order to maximize the persuasive potential of the closing argument, the lawyer needs to imbed the case story or continuity into the minds of the jurors while simultaneously maintaining their attention through the process.[35] It is the lawyer's job to tell the jury what the case was all about in clear, simple declarative phrases. Presented in this way, jurors will give their attention and focus to important points to follow.

When does closing argument matter? Research suggests that when neither side surpasses the other in the substance presented during the trial, when the lawyers are equally skilled, when the lawyers are equally prepared, and when the jury is balanced in its pre-existing attitudes, then closing argument is strongly influential on the ultimate verdict. Conversely, if one side has a much more solid case than the other, or where a lawyer is substantially more skilled than the other, where one lawyer is significantly more prepared than the other, or when the jury has

---

35   Richard J. Crawford. *The Persuasion Edge.* (New York: Wiley Press, 1989).

significantly tainted views, the closing argument can be of less import on jury decision making. On the other hand, where the lawyer reshapes evidence to fit the reality of the jurors, then the closing argument has a greater potential for impact. Persuasive power means reaching into the reality of the jurors and not attempting to fit the case into the lawyer's version of reality.

Lawyers cannot ignore what has transpired before the closing argument. They must deal with the evidence as it came in. The attorney then needs to properly translate the weight of the burden of proof. A lay juror is unfamiliar with terms like "the preponderance of the evidence" or "beyond a reasonable doubt." The attorney needs to explain the appropriate burden and explain the facts of the case in light of that burden. This is the time to pull it all together in an interesting, cohesive fashion.

A key function of the closing argument is to strike and reinforce the core message of the case. It is a time to renew the relationship and rapport developed throughout the course of the trial as the lawyer attempts to read the leaning of the jurors going into the closing argument. This needs to be accomplished within the structure of the jury instructions that guide the deliberations. Jurors, by definition and law, must follow and apply the instructions. The lawyer needs to retell the client's story in a manner that is not only complete, consistent, and coherent, but which also fits the letter of the law. You may recall the infamous Heidi Fleiss (Hollywood Madam) case, in which my office worked with the defense to select the jury. That case was going on at the same time as the O. J. Simpson case, and it garnered significant attention as well. One day I ran into my trial consulting partner, Richard Gabriel, who had selected the Fleiss jury. I asked him how things looked as the trial drew to a close, and he said that all was going to be just fine. Then the jury came back with a verdict of guilty. Richard knew something was wrong, as the sense of things in the courtroom was just not in the direction of guilt. With court permission, our office interviewed the jurors, and it came to light that the jury members admittedly misunderstood their role! They returned with a verdict of guilty, but such was not the intention of at least five jurors. Through these interviews and post-verdict motions, a new trial was ultimately granted. I wonder whether a more precise and carefully constructed closing argument for the defense would have led to a different verdict, freedom for Ms. Fleiss, the first time around.

Remember, the attorney is not confined to arguing only what is in evidence. Lawyers can address common sense and general knowledge and understanding, but they should also be cognizant of the legal jury instructions that jurors often use to guide their evaluation. It is important to be careful not to overreach or overstate the evidence. Overstating or misstating facts is a cardinal sin in the world of trial advocacy. This means lawyers must be fair in any attacks on the adversary's position and evidence. As you speak to a jury, consider the power of your gestures and their placement. Research shows that gestures placed close to the body and directly in front of you create the sense of present and current, while gestures that are made away from the body suggest distance in time and space. As your language points to the future care of a plaintiff in a personal injury case, for example, you may wish to place the need of such future care through gestures in the present tense (in front of you). The key is to remain conscious of the importance of gestural placement while presenting the closing argument. The fact that the need is in the future does not mean you need to place that need in the future; you may well want to create a current-time need through gestures close to and directly in front of your body.

Conclude the closing argument with confidence and eloquence. The final words should be powerful ones, ones that leave the jurors with a sense of commitment, direction, and certainty. Make it clear to the jurors what verdict you expect from them and ensure that your closing words bring together the story or continuity, theme, and message running throughout the trial. Remember that unlike direct and cross-examination, the lawyer is in total control during closing argument. It can be the most powerful moment, but it is a moment that should be planned, not from the onset of the trial, but from the beginning of the case. Look ahead from the first days the case comes to you through discovery to where you wish to end up in a closing argument. Enjoy the greater comfort you experience in closing argument when and if that moment of trial ultimately occurs by preparing effectively from the very first day you get the case. After all, aren't those great trial moments exactly what led you to become a trial lawyer in the first place?

PART VI.

BEYOND THE HALLS OF JUSTICE

LAWYER AS PUBLIC FIGURE

Beyond the courtroom, lawyers reach out into the public sector for a host of reasons. Whether to share technical expertise with colleagues at a continuing education program, a "beauty contest" presentation to a group of general counsel in the hope of new business, an invited appearance at a conference, or even a toast at a wedding, we often transfer our courtroom skills to a non-adversarial setting. This section explores the world of public speaking and also addresses one of the most challenging settings we lawyers can find ourselves in: the need to respond to or otherwise handle the media when we are involved in a high-profile matter.

A Fear Worse Than Death!

Public Speaking: the Number One Human Fear

Speaking in public can unravel even the most self-assured of us. Surveys of human fears consistently rank public speaking as the number-one fear, followed by the "lesser" fears of death and killer insect bites! If fact, even the late comedian George Jessel quipped, "The human brain is a wonderful organ. It starts to work as soon as you are born and doesn't stop until you get up to deliver a speech."

In my career as a public speaker for bar associations, corporations, and international conferences, and also as a coach for other professional speakers, including political candidates, I have learned that speaking in a public forum should be a most exciting and positive experience. You just have to combat the psychological fears that interfere with what would otherwise be a rewarding experience.

Public communication is clearly the most powerful and effective means of disseminating information and affecting the direction of people, organizations, and governments. Whether in court, in a continuing legal education program, or on a social occasion, most people desire to be effective when speaking in public. Many people have come to recognize the great responsibility we have to relate effectively with others in a public forum.

Success in public speaking rests in proper preparation, rehearsal, keeping some key delivery tips in mind, and, most important, adjusting the movie that runs through our heads that keeps trying to tell us over and over just how terrible the experience is going to be. Nothing can be further from the truth; we just have to make the shift internally. Simply put, for most people who fear public speaking, the resolution rests in their own minds. It is within their power to change.

Perhaps you haven't thought about it much, but you are guided and guarded by the pictures and movies that run in your head. These mental images that race through our heads constantly can be the source of our success or discomfort. Think about it. Perhaps you are afraid of flying or afraid of heights or have a fear of dogs. All these fears have one thing in common with public speaking: they live only in our minds. If you fear making a public presentation, it is likely because you see yourself over and over again failing in that presentation. Remember, this fear is only in your mind, but those internal images trigger the discomfort and nerves that truly block our effectiveness.

Do not underestimate the power of the unconscious. It is essential that you begin reducing and eliminating fear by changing the movies in your mind. By using the methods of information-processing adjustment, you can make permanent, positive changes in your life. I have worked with clients to help them eliminate their fears of flying, heights, and even public speaking. The amazing part is that for most people it takes less than thirty minutes to make the changes and eliminate the blocks.

There are some simple steps you can take to trigger some positive change. Start by seeing (truly visualizing) yourself succeeding in your own mind. See the audience enjoying your presentation, and experience the positive feelings associated with doing an excellent job. It may take some time to create permanent shifts; after all, the negative movies in your head have been embedded for years. But start the process of changing now.

You can't expect others to enjoy your presentation unless you believe yourself that it will be enjoyable and informative. Remember that others have come to hear what you have to say. If you are psyched to give the talk, and if you believe that what you have to say has value and interest to others, then you are on your way to making some positive change. In fact, doesn't it make sense to you that an audience *wants* you to be interesting and effective? No one wants to be bored, so we begin the public speaking event with listeners who have the desire to enjoy themselves.

Preparation is key to an effective presentation. Few speakers can be effective speaking off the cuff without proper research and organization. Some people can deliver a successful speech because they enjoy the experience themselves. The movie that runs in their mind is one of fun and enjoyment of public speaking, so that even an impromptu talk doesn't unnerve them. For most people, spending the time necessary to put together an excellent presentation will add a great deal to your confidence level.

Rehearsing the talk as part of your preparation is essential as well. Practice your presentation in front of friends or family members to gain positive feedback and suggestions on how you can improve the presentation. The more you rehearse your presentation, the more confidence you will gain. Each time you rehearse, add another step to that movie in your mind. See a successful presentation; see an audience that enjoys what you have to say; and notice how the nervous feeling subsides, replaced by a more positive energy.

On the day of your presentation, arrive early and check out the room. Arriving only moments before you have to speak creates enough stress to unnerve anyone. Visit the room, be sure it is set up as you wish, and be certain to check out the equipment. Use the microphone and the overhead projector, and stand on the podium, behind the lectern. Get a feel for the room and the experience. This will also add to your confidence level as you strengthen the movies in your mind about the public speaking experience.

When you make the presentation, keep some simple rules in mind. These items will seem like common sense, but they get violated by speakers all too often:

1. Don't apologize or complain to the audience—about anything. A speaker who complains about the room setup, temperature, refreshments, late start, early departure, or whatever, does little more than call the audience members' attention to something that may not have mattered to them in the first place. Simply begin, "Seeing

that we are beginning a bit later than scheduled, let's move right into the…"

2. Don't chew gum or ice at the microphone. I have actually seen speakers sip water and chew their ice cubes, letting the noise go right into the microphone. Keep everything out of your mouth except for some water if you must have some.

3. Use visual aids whenever possible. People's attention spans are short. You will capture their attention for longer periods of time if you use a PowerPoint presentation to enhance and support what you say. Most importantly, the PowerPoint slides will also serve as your speaking notes, so you may not need to have anything else in front of you as a crutch!

4. Begin with an appropriate attention-capturing introduction, and be sure to end with a summary of your main points. Avoid saying, "Well, I guess that's it," or "I'm done." Create closure by thanking the audience members for their attention or leaving them with a key thought or quote.

Powerful public presentations are clearly within your abilities. Rely on proper preparation, rehearsal, and a smart delivery, but most importantly begin by embedding the positive images of the public speaking experience in your mind… and enjoy the applause.

And Your Point Is? (Again)

Establishing Purpose in Public Presentations

A lawyer speaking in public has a purpose. Unlike the poet, artist, or composer who at times may create a work as a means of self-expression, the lawyer as public speaker often wants to trigger a specific response from the listener, be it a jury or other audience. What I have in mind for this chapter is the lawyer who speaks not only in court, but also at a continuing legal education function, a business development presentation (sometimes called a beauty contest), or some other event that brings the lawyer in front of an audience.

Historically grounded in rhetorical theory, there are three main purposes for speechmaking: to provide information, to persuade, and to entertain. Our focus on the lawyer in the courtroom (or other settings) suggests that entertainment is not typically the purpose or goal. It is fair to state, however, that a lawyer must be engaging if he or she hopes not to lose juror or other audience attention in the course of the trial or talk (perhaps CLE or business development).

When a lawyer's central purpose is to inform, then that lawyer wants to provide the audience with new information to clarify a concept, explain terms and relationships, clarify value, or otherwise widen the range of the audience's knowledge of the case at hand. The goal to inform assumes that the audience (jury or otherwise) has little, or at least insufficient knowledge of the subject. It is the lawyer as speaker's responsibility to ensure that the information disseminated is presented in such a way that jurors or others get the point. In the case of a jury, members' deliberations would better be guided by that information.

Following are a series of steps a lawyer can take to better ensure that information is retained by a jury or other audience:

1. Limit the amount of information presented, but expand the presentation of that information. For example, two thoughts explained through examples and illustrations will be better recalled than five thoughts listed without accompanying illustrative information.

2. Clarify and stress the relevance of the information presented to listeners' own backgrounds or existing knowledge base. Go further by establishing connections between the new information and the needs, wants, or goals of the audience.

3. Be certain to present information in a non-threatening manner, because most people are quickly turned off by speakers who are perceived in a negative way.

4. Be certain to present the information at a level appropriate for the audience; i.e., do not speak too simplistically if the audience is sophisticated or you may be perceived as patronizing. Similarly, attempts to impress a jury by speaking in technical terms will only serve to confuse and annoy that jury.

Essentially the speaker must know whether the presentation is of new information or is more of an informative briefing; i.e., to a group with some previous background on the topic. In the latter case, the lawyer may want to presume that the audience needs *no* basic information. If, however, the lawyer is mistaken in the assumption and the listeners do not have significant background and familiarity with the topic, the listeners may end up confused, and the lawyer's purpose is not met. In short, it is critical to make the effort to know the knowledge base of the audience.

Trial lawyers not only want to educate jurors (or other audiences, for that matter), they seek to persuade them as well. Persuasion can be defined as a conscious attempt by one person to modify or otherwise influence the perceptions and/or behaviors of another. In other words, a lawyer may wish to focus on listener attitude to obtain conviction or value re-evaluation, or on listener behavior if the object is to have the listener take an action step such as reach a specific verdict.

It is nearly impossible to separate the lawyer's impact on an audience, such as a jury, from the substance of the message itself. When jurors come to hold the lawyer in high regard, for example, they are more likely to adopt a more favorable attitude toward the propositions offered than if they develop a negative impression of that lawyer. Credibility can be broken down into five fundamental components: competence, trustworthiness or character, composure, sociability, and dynamism. Although credibility results from the combined impact of these variables, there is research to suggest that if the lawyer's character or trustworthiness is brought into question, then credibility is jeopardized. Accordingly, it is essential that the lawyer appear competent (often a result of the background and credentials set out in the introduction of that lawyer) and comfortable at the podium (composed and in control), and, above all, trustworthy and of good character.

The persuasive speech, taking the form of opening statement or closing argument or some other presentation, needs be structured in a way that will best accomplish the objective of the presentation. For example, if the lawyer determines that the jurors or other listeners are already in agreement with his or her point of view, then the speech may be structured deductively; that is, arguing from general to specific points. Conversely, if the jury or audience is in opposition to the lawyer as speaker's point of view, then the lawyer is better advised to structure the arguments inductively; i.e., taking listeners from specifics they can accept to a general conclusion with which they might agree.

The emotional climate of the audience refers to the pre-existing attitude of the audience members. Knowing the audience's predisposition toward the lawyer's presentation is critical for planning the strategy of the speech. Explanation of the lawyer as speaker's point of view may be necessitated in the event of a negative perception held by the audience.

The purpose or topic of the speech should be worthwhile, relevant, and interesting for both the audience and the lawyer as speaker. It is useful to develop a purpose statement that alerts the audience to the specific intentions of the speaker by informing listeners of what the speaker wants; i.e., whether the speaker wants the audience to gain information, change an attitude, or engage in a certain type of behavior. You can see how and why a lawyer must have a strong sense of purpose and mission as he or she plans the public presentation.

I'm the Press...
Trust Me!

Handling Trial Publicity and Reporters

<hr>

"Attorney Gassman, can you comment please on the impact of your recent loss at trial for your client who now faces life in prison?" Although a straightforward and seemingly nonjudgmental question, the response seems to get twisted, contorted, and turned inside out once it appears in print or on television. Why does a media interview, print or television, so often transform what seemed to be a wonderful opportunity to clarify an issue into an entangling mess from which we then must work to free ourselves?

A media interview can be the positive experience we want it to be, if we understand how to handle the interaction. Having personally faced reporters who twist words, promise to keep conversations off the record (but then do not), and appear to be supportive, I learned some important lessons in dealing with the media and am happy to share them. Save yourself the misery and turn the encounter into a positive one.

The media believes that impressions and judgments of a person are made within the first few seconds after he or she begins to speak. It is also true that reporters have a story in mind when they make the telephone call to you or send the camera crew to catch up with you. Given a reporter's power of the pen and the ability to edit videotape, the lawyer who agrees to an interview had better be prepared for the experience, if they hold out any hope to control the interaction.

Simply put, the power and influence of the media, not to mention the twenty-four-hour endless news cycle, has made being prepared a necessity for any lawyer who finds himself or herself in the public eye. The more successful and powerful you grow in the field, the more in demand as an interview subject you will find yourself to be, either because of your role in a specific matter or because of your expertise in the field in general.

A few summers ago, after an official news conference on a matter concluded, one reporter took me aside and asked, off-the-record, about my impressions of another lawyer. Knowing that there is no such thing as off-the-record in a media interview, I responded carefully and exercised great caution to say nothing that I thought could come back to haunt me, yet the article appeared the next day in national newspapers, and the reporter had done his best to integrate my off-the-record comments into the theme of the interview. When I called that reporter and challenged his violation of my off-the-record comments, he said there was no such thing as off-the-record for him, and he had to print what I said as part of the story. That's a reporter I will never assist again. The message is clear to us all: interviewee, beware!

Reporters often have a theme or point they seek to develop. It may be the subordination of justice, the fairness of the verdict, or the skill of a lawyer. Questions are often posed to explore or support that theme. Keep in mind that a print or on-air reporter would really like to break a story, or at least "make news." A reporter sent to cover a story seeks to write a unique and interesting account that will get a prime space in the publication or telecast. Whether the latest political election or the latest case of the century, a reporter is in a daily search for a headline or an angle. Reporters are trained to ask difficult questions and will persist even in the face of a "no comment," or other too-simple response. Where nothing more is offered, the reporter turns a "no comment" into news by focusing on that answer as news itself.

Recently I actually tried to help a reporter write a better and more accurate article. Called to get my opinion on who the desired jurors for the prosecution and defense would be in a high profile case, I told the reporter that while I know she wished me to give demographic information, that detail was not as meaningful as other life experience-relevant information. That is, whether a person is white or black, male or female, old or young is not as telling as the life experiences a person has, which informs their attitudes and values. I offered suggestions to the reporter on how best to present the information, and then the article was published. How was I quoted? By extracting those few words about gender and race that I said and leaving it at that. The reporter met her deadline and I got some publicity, but the readers were really cheated by not getting a fuller and more accurate view of the points I was trying to make. Such is the reality of media deadlines and space limitations

The secret to success in a media interview is shaping the encounter so it works to your advantage. Know that the reporter has done homework to learn what he or she can about you; you must prepare ahead of time, thinking ahead to what you would like the ultimate article or telecast to look like. When you know or suspect an interview is forthcoming, think ahead to the most difficult or embarrassing questions you can be asked and know your responses. You cannot win by looking flustered or angry on camera or in print.

When asked a difficult or loaded question, pause for a brief moment before responding. Give yourself the chance to select the proper words, because your words may very well end up becoming the headline of that story. You must do what the reporters have done: select a theme or message you wish to establish and do all you can do to control the message. Simply put, the effective media answer is stated in *your* words and on your terms. The best politicians learn this fact once they have had their fill of misquotes.

When asked a question, respond in stand-alone, complete sentences, those that establish the desired theme or purpose. When asked to "comment on your loss," understand that a response that is less than a complete sentence and full thought can and likely will be pulled out by the media for analysis. Thus "We did our best" may be edited out of a series of sentences and a more negative view is created with the edited quotes. You maintain better control if you give your response in complete sentences, fluently, and without much pause, so as to reduce the chance of midstream editing.

Consider the response: "Our strategy in this case was to set the facts out as they happened, and we hoped that the jury would see that the truth was on our side." This response, even if removed and placed elsewhere, cannot be transferred away from that lawyer's theme; therefore, the lawyer controls.

The interviewee's goal in responding to any question is to enlighten, not debate; to teach, not argue; to clarify, not defend. By maintaining this positive view of the media interview process, you can be much more assured of coming across in a desirable way. It may seem strange at first to speak in complete sentences in response to most questions and to supply a statement of policy in response to a yes or no question, but such is an approach of necessity if you are to control your media image.

I can recall a case a few years back where the plaintiff's lawyer was less than pleased with the verdict returned in an admitted liability case. Expecting an unwieldy sum (she asked the jury for more than $30 million), she was displeased when the jury returned a verdict for slightly more than $9 million; sizable, yes, but much smaller a verdict than sought or expected. In fact, under all legal accounts, the verdict was considered a defense victory. I recall that lawyer storming out of the courtroom and courthouse filled with anger and disappointment that the jurors could be, in her opinion, so wrong.

And yet that evening it was the plaintiff's lawyer who appeared on every newscast and was the one reporters sought out for the news. You see, the media was astounded that such a large sum was awarded (it was a record for its time); the media knew nothing of the potential sum that was demanded, expected, but not realized. The power of the media may never have been stronger in creating a media victory for that plaintiff's lawyer, who, incidentally, played up to the supportive theme offered for broadcast. Talk about turning a lemon into lemonade, this case produced a victory for the defense and defense firm, which had more than $90 million of insurance proceeds that could have been tapped into had the verdict been higher, and yet a verdict less than $10 million was heralded as a huge plaintiff's victory. Little did the media know that more had been offered in settlement than was returned by the jury.

Imagine if the lawyer had instead displayed displeasure. What public image would have been created then? That plaintiff's lawyer was brilliant to spin the verdict into a total win. In the court of public opinion it was a win, and that lawyer was rewarded with many new cases over subsequent years.

In summary, when provided with a media opportunity, always be certain you do the following:

- know your theme and message;
- pause before responding to select words that may become a headline; and
- speak in complete sentences that incorporate your theme and set out a positive statement of policy as you respond to the inquiry.

Appreciate the power of the media; do not underestimate its influence. Welcome the opportunity to establish a positive image and position, so long as you recognize your ability to control the substance of what you say. In the immortal words of the legendary newscaster Walter Cronkite, "And that's the way it is."

About the Author

Dr. Paul M. Lisnek is a nationally respected expert on communication, jury and trial dynamics, negotiation, and ethics. He is the cofounder and CEO of Decision Analysis, a leading trial consulting firm based in Los Angeles, Chicago, and San Francisco. The firm has worked in numerous high-profile cases, including O. J. Simpson, Whitewater, Phil Spector, Enron, and Firestone.

An Emmy, CableFax, and Beacon Award-winning television host, Dr. Lisnek currently anchors *Newsmakers* and *Political Update* and is the political analyst for WGN-TV and CLTV. Paul has served as a legal, political, and ethics expert for NBC, CNN,

ABC, and FOX, and appears often on *In Session*. He has been featured on numerous national television shows, including *The Today Show*, *NBC Nightly News*, *Fox Morning Live*, and *Anderson Cooper 360*. His radio presence includes host of *The Paul Lisnek Show* on WVON-AM and legal analyst for NPR's *Talk of the Nation*, *Canada AM*, and *The Verdict with Paula Todd*.

Dr. Lisnek is a frequent lecturer for the U.S. Department of Justice and its Justice Leadership Institute and at bar association and corporate meetings nationwide. Formerly the assistant dean and lecturer in law at Loyola Law School in Chicago, he has taught at the University of Illinois, DePaul University, and Pepperdine University School of Law's Institute for Dispute Resolution. Dr. Lisnek holds a PhD in speech communication in addition to his law degree, both from the University of Illinois.

Dr. Lisnek served two terms as president of the American Society of Trial Consultants, has served on the faculty of NITA, and is a commissioner and inquiry panel chairperson of the Illinois Attorney Disciplinary Commission, an Illinois Supreme Court appointment for which he was recently honored for over twenty years of service. He has several years' experience as an arbitrator and mediator.

A recognized expert in litigation skills, Dr. Lisnek has authored several articles and twelve other books, including *The Hidden Jury* (with foreword by the late Johnnie Cochran). Other titles include *Courtroom Power*; *Depositions*; *Negotiating Power*; and *The Lawyer's Handbook for Interviewing and Counseling*.

The author welcomes your thoughts, comments, and reactions. For more information or to contact the author, please visit **www.PaulMLisnek.com**.